IMAGES
of America

BOSTON'S
FINANCIAL DISTRICT

This view looks down Washington Street toward the Old South Meeting House at Milk Street. The former Marlborough Street was renamed in 1789 in honor of George Washington. By the late 19th century, it had become a busy thoroughfare with streetcars operating on all the major city streets, which connected the city to the outlying neighborhoods. Designed by Joshua Blanchard and built in 1729, the Old South Meeting House, or more correctly, the Third Church in Boston, is seen in the center of the photograph, with its wood steeple dominating the late-19th-century streetscape. The comparison between the Old South Meeting House and the commercial blocks creates an interesting juxtaposition between Colonial architectural details interspersed within the 19th-century streetscape of commercial and retail granite buildings. The streetscape includes Raymond's Department Store, seen on the right—a once famous department store that used Uncle Eph and Aunt Abby as its beloved trademark.

IMAGES
of America

BOSTON'S
FINANCIAL DISTRICT

Anthony Mitchell Sammarco

ARCADIA
PUBLISHING

ISBN 978-1-5316-0737-1

Published by Arcadia Publishing
Charleston, South Carolina

Library of Congress Catalog Card Number: 2002110445

For all general information contact Arcadia Publishing at:
Telephone 843-853-2070
Fax 843-853-0044
E-Mail sales@arcadiapublishing.com
For customer service and orders:
Toll-Free 1-888-313-2665

Visit us on the Internet at www.arcadiapublishing.com

The Old State House, built in 1711–1712 on the site of Boston's first town house and the 17th-century Haymarket, still commands a position of prominence at the head of State Street almost three centuries later. Here, an impressive 1801 painting depicting the head of State Street, which had been renamed in 1789 from King Street, shows the center of town and commercial Boston. The imposing First Church in Boston and its prominent octagonal belfry are located to the left of the Old State House. On the right, a man holds a horse in front of the former Royal Custom House, which had been referred to as Butchers' Hall by the patriots during the American Revolution and was labeled as such by Paul Revere in his historical print of the Boston Massacre. In the foreground is a horse-drawn stagecoach, which connected Boston to outlying towns on a regular schedule and was also transportation for citizens going about their daily business over two centuries ago. (Courtesy Massachusetts Historical Society collection.)

4

CONTENTS

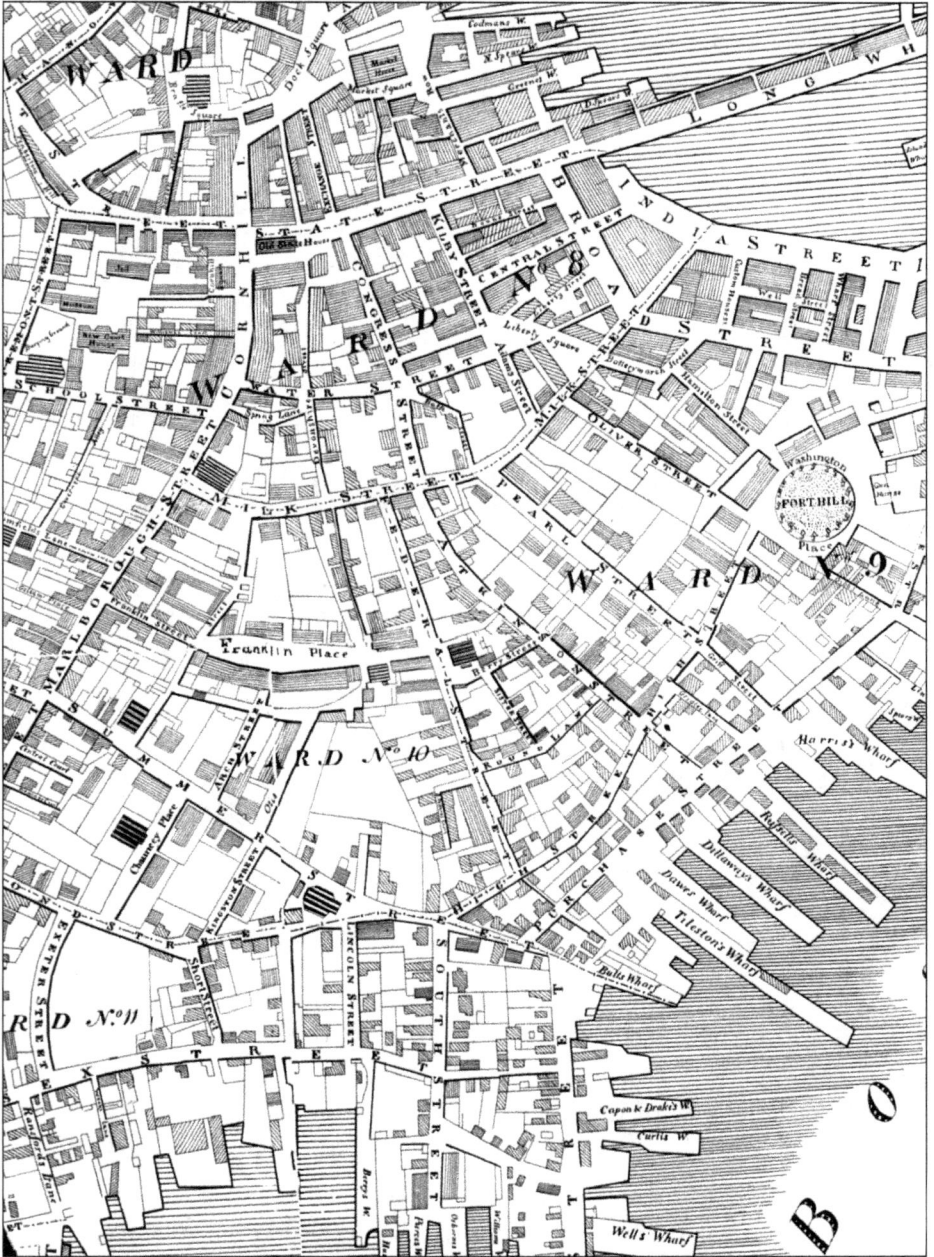

A detail drawing of the J.G. Hales map of Boston in 1814 shows the area of downtown Boston, with wards 7, 8, 9, 10, and 11 representing the area from Dock Square to the edge of the old South End with numerous wharves projecting into Boston Harbor along the waterfront. Hales was a geographer and surveyor, as well as a skilled cartographer, who detailed the town in the decade prior to its incorporation as a city in 1822. Much of the old South End, the area of Summer and Franklin Streets and the associated streets in the neighborhood, remained a desirable residential district well into the mid-19th century. By the time of the Civil War, however, it had been almost wholly given over to commercialism, and families dispersed to the new South End and Back Bay of the city.

INTRODUCTION

*Greatness in cities in America is too often associated with prodigious
commercial activity, miles of business blocks, fine new sixteen-story buildings,
the ceaseless strife of toiling thousands, and other features of a "boom."*

—An astute anonymous observer in 1892

Boston's financial district is roughly bounded by Tremont, Essex, Court, and State Streets and the waterfront. Today, it is home to many leading banking and investment houses that transact business throughout the world. However, in the first two centuries after Boston was settled in 1630 by English Puritans seeking to create a new Zion in the Massachusetts Bay Colony, this area was a combination of residential land and small shops that would remain as such until the mid-19th century. By the time of the Civil War, Boston was deeply involved in the vast infilling project of the Back Bay, which took place after 1858. Thanks to the ingenious engineer John Souther and his "Souther steam shovel," one of the country's quintessential Victorian neighborhoods was ultimately created. As the residents of such streets as Summer, Kingston, Otis, Pearl, and High Streets in the old South End left their enclaves for the newly developed South End, the downtown area would become decidedly commercial with new business blocks of four- and five-story structures rapidly built to replace the former mansions.

Following the Civil War, Boston saw a dramatic decrease in all aspects of maritime commerce as the economy shifted toward the more lucrative manufacturing centers of Lowell and Lawrence, which produced cotton textiles that served the consumer base of the United States. The towns founded by Francis C. Lowell and Abbott Lawrence, two prominent Bostonians, used the waterpower afforded by the Merrimac River. Their extensive mills were staffed with both native Americans and an ever increasing flow of immigrants, most of whom were from western Europe. However, downtown Boston was to eventually become a beacon that attracted businessmen who sought to succeed in business, finance, insurance, and trading concerns. Thereby, a center of finance in New England was created.

It was said in 1892 that "in its commercial, as distinguished from its aesthetic, aspect, Boston still occupies relatively as prominent a position among the cities as she ever did. While it is true that other cities in certain directions are growing more rapidly, yet, in many instances, it is Boston brains and Boston capital and Boston methods which are reasonable for their advancement." In the 1875–1900 period, Boston's banking and investment houses expanded to provide services for the up-and-coming middle class investor who "stands in the forefront in developing property and otherwise affording opportunities for commercial prosperity." It was in Boston that life insurance began, as well as superior carriers of fire insurance. Following the Great Boston Fire of 1872, the number of manufacturing industries located in the city numbered in the hundreds and included the boot and shoe industry, the leather, cotton, and wool exchanges, publishing houses, and impressive retail houses, most of which were located in the financial district. One newspaper wag said it was the "east wind, a codfish diet, and other innocent fictions" that accounted for the causes of intellectual Boston people, but only to those of the manor born! Boston was referred to as the "Athens of America," and even more boldly, as the "Hub of the Universe" by Oliver Wendell Holmes, who portrayed Boston as an intellectual hotbed of thinkers, movers, and shakers who, with the new business lords in Boston's financial district, made Boston home not just to the bean and the cod but to a wide spectrum of people who originally hailed from every corner of the earth.

In the period between World War II and the present, Boston's financial district has gone from the Boston Custom House—the only high-rise office building in this area of Boston—to a multitude of skyscrapers that now blanket the district. Beginning in the 1930s with the Batterymarch Building (60 Batterymarch Street) and the United Shoe Machinery Building (138–164 Federal Street), the massive rebuilding of the financial district continued in the 1960s with the New England Merchants National Bank (28 State Street), the Boston Company Building (1 Boston Place), the First National Bank of Boston Building (99 High Street), State Street Bank Building (225 Franklin Street), and the Shawmut Bank (1 Federal Street). The rebuilding seemingly continues unabated to this day. In the last decade, the area that once had elegant Federal mansions and verdant gardens with views of the sea has given way to a densely built-up commercial area with a multitude of buildings and commercial concerns, creating a thriving nexus of businesses. The last two centuries in the history and development of Boston's financial district have seen tremendous changes and usages, which will probably continue in the next two centuries.

Still, this vibrant and energetic area of the city of Boston draws businesspeople, clients, tourists, and native Bostonians alike to the financial center of the "Hub of the Universe."

The city of Boston was incorporated in 1822. After that time, it began to see tremendous topographical changes with the cutting down of the three hills known as the Trimount—Mount Vernon and Beacon and Pemberton Hills—and the infilling of the waterfront around Dock Square. Here, in an 1850 print, the Boston Custom House has been built on India Street at the head of Long Wharf, where the bowsprits of packet ships practically came up to the granite steps and where they discharged their cargo for distribution to vendors in the city. Today, the area is hemmed in on all sides by development. The impressive custom house was designed by Ammi Burnham Young, who was assisted by J.H. Hammatt Billings. It was built between 1837 and 1849 of Quincy granite, and a tower designed by Peabody & Stearns was built in 1915.

One

THE OLD SOUTH END

In the early 19th century, the South End of Boston was a fashionable residential district with impressive mansions, tree-lined streets, and lavish gardens. The streets such as Summer, Franklin, Otis, High, and Pearl Streets were lined with imposing brick mansions, many of which were designed by Boston's "gentleman architect" and native-born son Charles Bulfinch (1763–1848). Beginning in the 1790s, the Harvard College–educated Bulfinch, following a grand tour of Europe, began transforming the town of Boston from a small, provincial seaport to an urbane and sophisticated city of brick and granite buildings. Starting in 1793 with the design and construction of the Tontine Crescent on Franklin Street, Boston's architectural outlook was to be vastly broadened by Bulfinch's astute perspective and obviously perceptive neoclassical designs. He was to serve as chairman of the selectmen of Boston and oversee the implementation of new architectural perspectives and how they ultimately changed the face of the old town. Between 1793 and 1820, he would lay the underpinnings of what would become the city of Boston in 1822 and the gateway to 19th-century architectural, topographical, and ethnic changes that would radically transform Boston into the Athens of America and, as it was later coined by Oliver Wendell Holmes, "the Hub of the Universe." In the first two decades of the 19th century, the Old South End had become the most fashionable residential area in town with close proximity to the waterfront and breathtaking views of the harbor from Fort Hill, a one-time fortified eminence.

The Vassall-Gardner House once stood on Summer Street between Chauncey and Washington Streets. Built in 1727, it was typical of early-18th-century wood houses in Boston that were set in a fenced, well-kept garden. The house is seen here just prior to its demolition in 1854 to make way for a commercial block built by the Gardner family. The still well-tended Colonial house had a large carriage house set at the end of a cobblestone drive. The crenellated tower seen in the distance is that of the Church of Our Savior (organized in 1845), which was designed by J.H. Hammatt Billings and built on Bedford Street. The house was a poignant reminder of the once common pre-Revolutionary streetscapes in town, and it would remain a remarkably long time into the 19th century. Today, Macy's occupies its site.

The view from Fort Hill in the early 19th century was spectacular, as the hill was 100 feet high. Accessible from Milk, Broad, and, High Streets, the area was developed with a circle of respectable mansions facing a circular green that was enclosed by a cast-iron fence. Although a secluded neighborhood, it attracted numerous residents who often wandered to the crest of the hill in the early summer evenings to enjoy the views and cool breezes. In this print, a corner of a rowhouse can be seen on the left, with cows grazing on the green and a man looking through a telescope on the right. The town lies in the distance, and the Park Street Church, the Old State House, the Old South Meeting House, and the Old North Church can be seen rising above the houses and shops.

The Dalton House was set in a large garden at the corner of Congress and Water Streets. Built in 1758 by Capt. Timothy Dalton, the three-story house was typical of houses in the Old South End in the 18th century. Congress Street, today a major street in the financial district, was a combination of Atkinson and Dalton Streets and was renamed in 1854.

Upon its completion in 1808, the Boston Exchange Coffee House was probably the most impressive building ever built in Boston. Seen here in a woodcut by Abel Bowen, it was built at the corner of Congress and State Streets, facing Congress Square. The building was seven stories in height with a center dome and cost a mind-boggling $500,000. It was the leading hotel in town, with a reading room, a drawing room, and a dining room that could seat 300 diners. In 1817, accommodations for the 11 Masonic bodies in Boston were provided here, and their lodges were elegantly furnished. However, all of this elegance was destroyed in a fire in 1818. On the far left can be seen the spire of the Old South Meeting House.

11

Scion of the prominent Apthorp and Bulfinch families, Charles Bulfinch was destined for the life of a gentleman. However, his projected Franklin Street development, known as the Tontine Crescent, forced him into bankruptcy and the need to view architecture as a remunerative career. Although unfortunate for Bulfinch, this change in thinking was Boston's immense gain. He "was not an architect in the modern sense, he was an artist and had mastered some of the principles of his calling." Bulfinch served as a selectman of Boston between 1789 and 1793, serving as chairman from 1797 to 1818, in addition to being the chief of police.

The Tontine Crescent was a 240-foot row of houses designed by Charles Bulfinch and built between 1791 and 1795 as the first connected houses in Boston. Built of brick, the rowhouses shared a uniform setback from the street and roofline. The facades were painted grey to emulate Portland stone with white trim. The second floor of the central pavilion held the headquarters of the Boston Library Society, while the third floor housed the Massachusetts Historical Society. The locations were convenient, as many of the neighborhood residents patronized both. In the center of the 300-foot-long elliptical green was a large stone urn surmounting a plinth base that Bulfinch had brought back from England and placed there in memory of Benjamin Franklin (1706–1790), for whom the street had been named. After 1858, when the area was rebuilt with granite commercial buildings, the urn was placed on the Bulfinch family lot at Mount Auburn Cemetery in Cambridge.

The center pavilion of the Tontine Crescent was flanked on either side by eight three-story rowhouses and shared the same classical details. The archway was a convenient passage that led to Summer Street and eventually gave its name to Arch Street. On the second floor of the pavilion were once located the Boston Library Society (founded in 1794 and now a part of the Boston Athenaeum) and the Massachusetts Historical Society (founded in 1791 and located in the attic from 1794 to 1833). Today, the gentle curve of Franklin Street is perpetuated and echoes back two centuries to the elegant rowhouses.

In this view looking east from Washington Street, Franklin Place is on the left of the center green and Franklin Street is on the right. Four duplex houses of the same painted brick stood in an even row, facing Franklin Place, which is on the opposite side of the center green from the Tontine Crescent.

13

The four duplex rowhouses on Franklin Place shared the same neoclassical design as the Tontine Crescent, with elegant arcaded windows on the ground floor and Corinthian pilasters ornamenting the facades.

One of the more fashionably elegant residents of Franklin Place was Louisa Carolina Matilda Stoughton, the daughter of Don Juan Stoughton, Spanish consul in Boston. Depicted in 1794 by Gilbert Stuart as a lady of high fashion, she lived with her family at 24 Franklin Place, a Bulfinch-designed rowhouse facing the Tontine Crescent. She was married at the age of 16 to Don Josef de Jaudenes y Nebot, who arrived in the country in 1791 as Spanish chargé d'affaires. The fashionable couple returned to Majorca, Spain, where they lived an equally sumptuous lifestyle. (Courtesy Metropolitan Museum of Art collection.)

The Boston Theatre, designed by Charles Bulfinch, was built in 1794 at the corner of Federal and Franklin Streets, opposite the fashionable Tontine Crescent, seen on the left. An elegant building with an impressive arcaded facade, it was said at the time of its construction to have been "the most imposing theatre in the United States." The theater had a projecting arcaded portico that was surmounted by four Corinthian columns supporting a pediment. Theater patrons entered the foyer, which opened onto two rows of boxes on the second floor and a pit and gallery below. The theater was both elegant and spacious and had a ballroom and several retiring rooms for patrons.

The Boston Theatre was enjoyed for only four years, as it was destroyed by fire in 1798. Since theater was still frowned upon in Boston in the late 18th century, the destruction was said to be divine retribution. The theater was promptly rebuilt, although in a less elegant manner, with a design by Charles Bulfinch. Known as the Federal Street Theatre, it would eventually be called the Odeon Theatre until its demolition for a commercial block in 1852.

The Church of the Holy Spirit stood adjacent to the Tontine Crescent. Dedicated on September 29, 1803, on the east end of the fashionable rowhouses, the church had a simple yet elegant design that used the neoclassical design and colors of the Tontine Crescent. The church was elevated to that of a cathedral in 1808, when Father de Cheverus was made the first bishop of Boston. The cathedral was used as a place of worship by the Roman Catholics of Boston until 1860, when the increasingly commercial aspect of the downtown caused the archdiocese to sell the land to Isaac Rich. The archdiocese soon purchased land in Boston's South End and commissioned noted architect Patrick Keeley to design the present cathedral of the Holy Cross, which was consecrated in 1875. The spire of the Federal Street Church, designed by Charles Bulfinch and built in 1809, can be seen on the left. This church later moved in 1859 to the Back Bay and became known as the Arlington Street Church.

Jean-Louis A.M. LeFebvre de Cheverus (1768–1836) was the first Catholic bishop in Boston. Exiled from France during the French Revolution, he came to America and was immediately welcomed, due in part to his engaging personality and simple piety that was to bring ecumenical understanding in Boston. He raised sufficient funds, largely through the Protestant residents of the town, including Pres. John Adams, to commission Charles Bulfinch to design the Church of the Holy Cross. The church was built in 1803 on Franklin Street at the east end of the Tontine Crescent and opposite the Boston Theatre. (Courtesy Boston Museum of Fine Arts collection.)

The duplex Welles-Gray House was built c. 1812 for the Welles and Gray families at the corner of Summer and Kingston Streets. Sharing a common wall, the duplexes were mirror images of each other, built of red brick with elegant neoclassical details, such as paired columns, recessed window surrounds, and cast-iron balconies.

The Tappan House was an elegant three-story house designed by Charles Bulfinch and built in 1798 at the corner of Summer and Arch Streets. John Tappan was a wealthy merchant who commissioned Bulfinch to build a house similar to the first house of Harrison Gray Otis, which still stands at the corner of Cambridge and Lynde Streets in the West End of Boston. A symmetrical house built of brick, it had a demilune window in the center of the third floor and a low hip roof.

The Everett House was half of a duplex house on Summer Street next to the Tappan House. Edward Everett (1794–1865) was a prominent resident of the Old South End in his retirement, although he was born in Dorchester, where his family had moved in the late 18th century. An eloquent speaker, he was a famous orator of the 19th century and is probably best known for his Gettysburg Address. A president of Harvard College, he also served as senator and congressman, as well as minister to the Court of St. James.

The First Church in Boston was founded in 1632. This photograph shows the third edifice, designed by architect and author of *The American Builder's Companion*, Asher Benjamin (1773–1845), and built in 1808 on Chauncey Street, near Summer Street. The church had been located in the State Street area for almost two centuries when the parishioners decided to move to the fashionable South End. Seen *c.* 1865, the church would later move to Boston's Back Bay when a new Victorian church of Roxbury puddingstone was designed by Ware & Van Brundt. Seen here, Chauncey Hall School is on the left of the church and the Massachusetts Charitable Mechanic Association, which was designed by J.H. Hammatt Billings and built in 1860, is on the right. In the distance is Summer Street with the commercial buildings encroaching upon the area in this decade. Today, Macy's and the Suissotel occupy the site.

The New Old South Church was designed by Charles Bulfinch and built of hammered Chelmsford granite in 1814. It is said to be the first church in Boston built of hammered granite. Built at the intersection of Bedford and Summer Streets, it gave the name Church Green to the small fence-enclosed grass plot once in front of it, and the intersection has been known as such ever since. One of numerous churches in the area, the Octagonal Church, as it was referred to in relation to its design, had a colonnade of fluted Doric columns and a graceful spire that dominated the area until the commercial encroachments caused its parishioners to move to other parts of the city. The church was demolished in 1868, after which it was replaced by a commercial block called the Church Green Building.

The interior of the New Old South Church was typical of the early 19th century, with a mahogany pulpit flanked by galleries Once described as being beautiful, as well as "light, rich, [and] well proportioned," it had Ionic columns and pilasters supporting arches with a gallery on three sides.

The Daniel Webster House was at the corner of Summer and High Streets. The great statesman—although born in Marshfield, where he kept an extensive estate—lived in the old South End.

Fort Hill, seen in the years just prior to the Civil War, was once a fortified hill but had become developed in the early 19th century with brick rowhouses surrounding a cast-iron-fenced circular green. The panoramic views of Boston Harbor from this elevated prominence must have been breathtaking. By the 1860s, the once fashionable area had become lodgings and tenements in an increasingly commercial district. In 1869, the hill was systematically leveled by 100 feet, with the fill being used to develop Atlantic Avenue and Church Street in Bay Village.

Two

A CITY EMERGES

Boston was incorporated as a city on March 4, 1822. The voters of Boston met at Fanueil Hall, where town meetings had been held since it was given to the town from benefactor Peter Fanueil, Esq., and voted in the affirmative to incorporate Boston as a city with a mayor and nine aldermen to administer the city. The first mayor of Boston was John Phillips (1822), a wealthy resident of Beacon Hill, followed by Josiah Quincy (1823–1828) and Harrison Gray Otis (1829–1831). In less than a decade, these three men, between 1822 and 1831, transformed the town into a thriving metropolis that earned the appellation of "the Athens of America."

Between 1822 and 1826, tremendous changes took place in the Dock Square area of the city through the infilling of the waterfront for new streets and the impressive Quincy Market, which stretched eastward from Fanueil Hall. Designed by Alexander Parris, Quincy Market was built of Quincy granite and designed in the then popular Greek Revival style of architecture, which was suited to being built in granite. Between the time Boston became a city and the Civil War, the entire financial district had become a thriving business district and the municipal pride of the city. The city local architects designed buildings that created not just architecturally important statements but ornaments to the city. Such buildings as St. Paul's Church (1819), Quincy Market (1824–1826), the Merchants Exchange (1842), the Bunker Hill Monument (1825–1843), and the Boston Custom House (1837–1849) were built. Each of these buildings, or monuments, was built of granite and was not just a permanent structure but an ornament to the city.

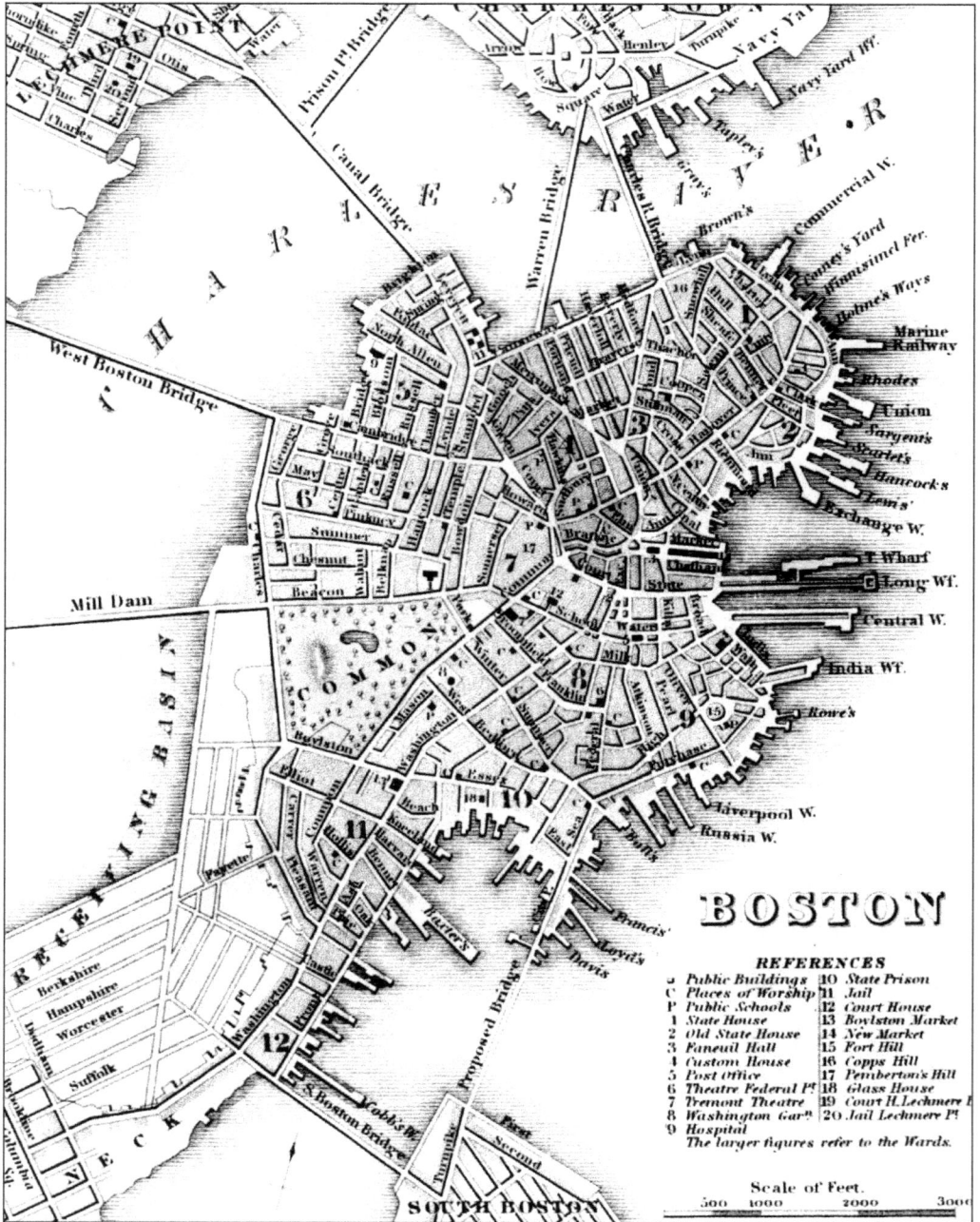

A detail drawing of an 1833 map of Massachusetts and Rhode Island by H.S. Tanner, who published *The Universal Atlas* in Philadelphia, shows the city a decade after its incorporation. Tremendous development occurred on either side of the old Colonial "neck of Boston," seen to the lower left, with the creation of the New South End. To the upper left is the receiving basin, which had already seen the beginning of the public garden adjacent to Boston Common and which, after 1858, was to become the massive infilling project of Boston's Back Bay. The city was accessible by bridges on the south, west, and north and had in 1804 annexed the former Dorchester Neck, seen to the lower right, renaming it South Boston.

A view looking toward the Old State House in 1849 shows State Street rebuilt with brick and granite commercial buildings. Located on the right of the Old State House is the United States Bank, which had been designed by J. H. Hammat Billings with an impressive colonnade of Ionic columns. To the right is the granite Union Block with the three arcaded windows, and to the far right is the impressive Ionic-columned Suffolk Bank. In the foreground is a horse-drawn two-wheeled street-watering cart that kept the dust down on the streets of the city and was in use well into the 20th century.

Located near the junction of Beacon and School Streets, Tremont Street was a busy intersection, as seen in this 1843 print. In the center is King's Chapel, which was designed by the English architect Peter Harrison (1716–1775) and built of Quincy granite. Fiske Kimball said Harrison's "buildings were exceptional in the America of that time for their purity of detail and their monumental qualities." The Ionic-columned portico, however, was designed by Charles Bulfinch and built in 1789. On the left is the Tremont House, and on the right the Tremont Theatre, both of which were designed by Isaiah Rogers (1800–1869). The Tremont Theatre was built in 1827 and was the second theater in Boston. In 1842, the building was sold to a Baptist congregation, which renamed the building the Tremont Temple Baptist Church.

Fanueil Hall was designed by the Scottish artist and architect John Smibert (1684–1751) and was built in 1742. A gift to the town for a marketplace and meeting hall from wealthy merchant Peter Fanueil, it was built on the edge of Boston's waterfront at Dock Square. This print depicts the marketplace prior to 1805, when it was doubled in size by Charles Bulfinch. In 1827, the first floor was divided into eight stalls, with occupants such as Milton & Slocumb (clothiers), Bass (hatter), and McElroy (iron and hardware) among the first occupants. On the right can be seen the streets and houses of the old Brattle Square area of town, which was swept away in the 1960s, when Boston City Hall and the plaza were laid out.

Peter Fanueil (1700–1743) was a Huguenot who had left France after the revocation of the Edict of Nantes. He eventually came to Boston, where he became a wealthy merchant whose mansion was built on Cotton (later Pemberton) Hill. His generosity to his fellow citizens in the gift of a marketplace and meeting hall was greatly appreciated, and the building has henceforth been known for the benevolent donor.

The Old Feather Store was located in Dock Square, with the waterfront directly behind the store. Built in 1680, the Old Feather Store was once the fashionable home of Thomas Staniford. The house was built of wood with a stucco covering and had numerous gables and an overhanging second floor. In 1820, the building became the store of John K. Simpson Jr., who sold feathers, mattresses, and bed ticking. Later in the 19th century, it was used by Charles J. Lovejoy, who operated a clothing warehouse.

Dock Square is shown in the area that includes the Old Feather Store and Fanueil Hall. Quincy Market is shown in the distance. The waterfront once came up to the area and was infilled in the early 19th century.

Fanueil Hall was greatly enlarged in 1805, when Charles Bulfinch doubled the size of the building and added a third floor. Surmounting the cupola is a copper grasshopper weathervane that was wrought by Dea. Shem Drowne in 1742. It has watched an ever changing town evolve into a city and the Dock Square area into one of the most heavily visited tourist attractions in the country. The third floor has been occupied by the armory of the Ancient and Honorable Artillery Company for many years, and it is where they maintain a museum.

The interior of Fanueil Hall contains a large two-story meeting place that has Doric columns supporting a gallery with Ionic columns above. Here, visitors marvel at the place often called "the Cradle of Liberty," where fiery orations were delivered during the Revolution. From the time it was built in 1742, all town meetings were held in the second-floor hall, as well as public demonstrations, receptions to distinguished guests and visitors to Boston, banquets, and balls. On March 4, 1822, the voters of Boston met in Fanueil Hall and voted to create the city of Boston.

A band poses for a group photograph during the 50th anniversary of the opening of Quincy Market in 1876. The festivities were led by Brown's Brigade Band, whose members are seen here lined up in regimental fashion. Many of the stallholders and Mayor Samuel Crocker Cobb (who served from 1874 to 1876) paraded around the market with great éclat. A large crowd gathered to watch the festivities and can be seen lining South Market Street, with the South Market on the left and Quincy Market on the right.

Josiah Quincy (1772–1864) was elected the second mayor of Boston, serving from 1823 to 1829. His portrait, by Gilbert Stuart, shows him appropriately seated in front of the temple-fronted west end of Quincy Market, which was designed by Alexander Parris and built of Chelmsford granite on the edge of the former Dock Square. Quincy was a visionary and, although opposed by a group of Bostonians, pressed forward with Parris in the creation of new streets and a sanitary marketplace that would provide ample supplies of produce, meats, and provisions, which were replenished daily. Once said to have "invested the sluggish town with new life, and brought into practical use a new watchword, Progress," Quincy was later to serve as president of Harvard College.

Alexander Parris (1780–1852) was the successor architect to Charles Bulfinch and literally built in granite what Bulfinch had built in brick. A native of Maine, he was a self-trained architect who used many of the new design books available for builders, such as Nicholson's *Principles of Architecture*. Among his notable buildings in Boston are St. Paul's Church on Tremont Street, Quincy Market, and the Sears House (now the Somerset Club) on Beacon Hill. Benjamin later published his own design book, *The Builder's Companion*, which was used by a generation of up-and-coming mid-19th-century architects and builders.

Quincy Market, officially known as Fanueil Hall Market, is a massive 535-foot-long granite building. Numerous delivery wagons are gathered near the west entrance to the market in this 1865 photograph. Both the west and east ends of the market had impressive porticos of bold Doric columns of Chelmsford granite supporting a pediment, with the walls made of Quincy granite. On the left, Fanueil Hall marks the western side of Fanueil Hall Square, the area between the two markets. In the distance can be seen the area of Brattle Street, which is now the site of Boston City Hall and its extensive plaza. (Courtesy William Varrell.)

The interior of Quincy Market has Doric columns that create a dual colonnade, which runs the length of the market. The market was 512 feet long and divided into 128 stalls with a center hall having a 46-foot-high dome supported by four segmental arches with panels and rosettes ornamenting its cove. With sides of meat hanging from hooks and sawdust-strewn floors, as seen in this 1870 photograph, the market was quite different than it is today with throngs of tourists and native Bostonians alike filling the food and souvenir booths. The sign suspended from the heating pipe in the center reads, "Smoking and Peddling Prohibited By Law within the Market." (Courtesy William Varrell.)

The South Market flanked Quincy Market with a row of offices and warehouses that shared a uniform granite post, as well as a lintel facade and roof with regimented dormer windows. Here were the famous Cottrell's Dining Room and Durgin Park Restaurant, which were patronized by market workers, businessmen, and tourists alike—all sitting at communal tables covered in red checked tablecloths. Here, numerous wagons are being unloaded with fresh fruits and vegetables along with barrels of every imaginable commodity. Notice the oyster bar on the far left—a small wood partition erected adjacent to the granite market where fresh oysters on the half shell were available at all times of the day and night for a quick snack. The North and South Markets were restored by F.A. Stahl & Associates.

An impressive and monumental building that took 12 years to complete, the Boston Custom House was built at the head of Long Wharf on the edge of Boston Harbor, where ships would actually come up to the building's granite stairs. Ammi Burnham Young created the quintessential Greek temple with 32 monolithic Doric columns on the exterior and interior rotunda of 12 marble Corinthian columns that supported a cornice upon which the center dome was set. The Roman dome was 25 feet in diameter and was sheathed with wrought-granite tiles, all of which were provided from the granite dressing sheds overseen by Gridley Bryant in East Milton.

The Boston Custom House, seen from India Street, shows the impressive granite Greek Cross Building before the tower was added in 1915, which replaced the central dome. The granite Doric columns were carved from solid pieces of Quincy granite. Each exterior Doric column weighs 42 tons and was brought from East Milton by teams of oxen with only one mishap—and that column was retrieved after the winter snows had melted and was erected on the exterior of the building.

Joy's Building, one of Boston's first office buildings, was built in 1809 at Cornhill Square. The section of Washington Street between School and Court Streets was referred to as Cornhill and is reinforced by the numerous bookstores and publishers, among them Coles Education Book Store, shown on the left. Joy's Building, a four-story brick commercial building with a center dome, had numerous businesses, such as Rodgers' Imperial Stock Linens, Casas' Drawing Academy, Williams' Boots & Shoes, Warren Shawls & Silks, as well as the Baptist Missionary Rooms. (Courtesy Boston Athenaeum collection.)

Boston's courthouse was designed by Charles Bulfinch as an impressive octagonal pavilion surmounted by a belfry with flanking wings on either side. Built in 1810 of Chelmsford granite, the building was often referred to as Johnson Hall in regards to Isaac and Lady Arabella Johnson, who owned the land in 1630. The Johnsons arrived in the country with John Winthrop, who, with the Puritans, settled Boston. After 1840, the building would become Boston's city hall. Eventually, it was demolished to make way for the present Old City Hall, which was designed by Gridley J. Fox Bryant and Arthur Gilman and completed in 1865.

The Old South Meeting House was designed by Joshua Blanchard and built in 1729. This was the third church in Boston (after First Church and the Old North Church) and was so named as it was in the South End of Boston. On the left is the Old South Building (designed by Arthur H. Bowditch and built in 1902–1904), which replaced a row of early granite-faced buildings.

Full sevenscore years our city's pride,
the comely southern spire
Has cast its shadow, and defied
the storm, the foe, the fire.

—Oliver Wendell Holmes

St. Paul's Church was designed by Alexander Parris and built in 1819 on Tremont Street, opposite the Boston Common. An impressive temple-fronted granite church, it has six Potomac sandstone Ionic columns carved by Solomon Willard (1783–1861) supporting a pediment. Stone was left in the tympanum for a bas-relief of *Paul Before Agrippa*, which was unfortunately never carved due to economic reasons. Built on Tremont Street between Winter and West Streets, this was a residential area in the early 19th century. The church interior was remodeled by Cram & Ferguson between 1913 and 1927.

Trinity Church, organized in 1723 and still the oldest Episcopalian church in the city, was designed by George Brimmer and built in 1829 at the corner of Summer and Hawley Streets. Built of massive rough-hewn granite blocks "in a solid Gothic [style of architecture] it was intended to reproduce the old English type of Episcopal temple with a squat crenellated tower." In the distance can be seen the spire of the Park Street Church, designed by Peter Banner and built in 1809 at the corner of Tremont and Park Streets. The parish worshiped here until 1872, when the church was destroyed in the Great Boston Fire. However, they had already purchased a large lot in the Back Bay, where H.H. Richardson was designing a new church.

The Masonic Temple was designed by Richard Bond and built of triangular pieces of granite that were quarried in Quincy in 1831. The temple was built at the corner of Tremont Street and Temple Place, adjacent to St. Paul's Church. An impressive crenellated twin-towered building with obelisk-like pinnacles, it was used by the Masonic fraternities in the city until 1858, when the building was sold to the federal government and was converted for use as a municipal courthouse. After 1885, the building was enlarged by two stories and thereafter used for business purposes. The impressive twin-towered building was later to be replaced by the R.H. White Department Store, which was designed by the Boston architectural firm of Parker, Thomas & Rice. It is now used for shops on the first floor with senior housing on the upper floors.

The Merchants Exchange was designed by Isaiah Rogers (1800–1869) and built in 1842 on State Street for the Boston Board of Trade. Built of Quincy granite, the exchange had six monumental Corinthian pilasters supporting a pediment with a tiered cupola from which a flagpole had been erected. In addition to serving as the financial center of the city, the exchange was also the site of the post office until it was moved to Post Office Square in 1873. To the right are the Tremont Bank and the Boston Bank Note Company, as well as many small businesses. (Courtesy Boston Athenaeum collection.)

The Merchants Exchange was designed by Isaiah Rogers and built in 1842 on State Street. Shown here in a close-up of the severely plain facade, the building was among the most impressive structures built in Boston of Quincy granite. The facade had six monumental engaged Corinthian pilasters, each of which was 45 feet high and weighed 55 tons. The pilasters supported a pediment and carved lintels with amphimion detailing, as well as a carved granite panel above the front entrance that was composed of a terrestrial globe surmounted by an American eagle.

The Massachusetts Horticultural Society built its first headquarters on School Street. The building, designed by Isaiah Rogers, was built in 1844 of Quincy granite. The temple-fronted building had a central oculus surmounting the roof and four Corinthian pilasters supporting a pediment. On the first floor can be seen the awning shading the society's seed store, where hybridized seeds of new strains of vegetables and flowers were sold to the public. The second floor had a large exhibition hall where fruits and flowers were displayed by proud members in weekly shows, which were well attended by members and friends. The exhibitions became so popular by the 1850s that large tents were erected on Boston Common for the displays.

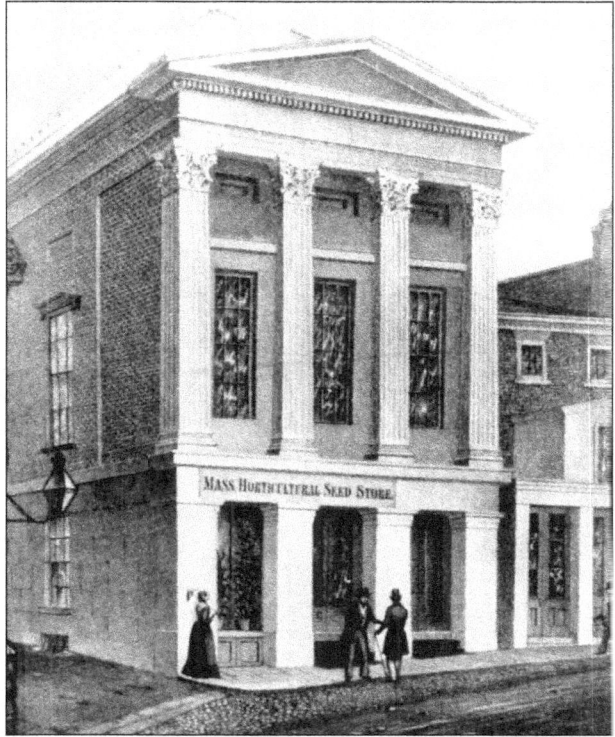

Henry A.S. Dearborn (1784–1851) was the first president of the Massachusetts Horticultural Society. He was a resident of Roxbury, where his estate, Datchet House, was on the eastern slope of Parker Hill at the corner of Tremont and St. Alphonsus Streets. The estate had extensive gardens and fruit orchards. Dearborn served as the second mayor of Roxbury (1847–1851), an independent city that was annexed to Boston in 1868. He was instrumental in the laying out in 1848 of Forest Hills Cemetery, an arboretum cemetery similar to Mount Auburn Cemetery in Cambridge and where he was buried on Dearborn Hill. His estate later became the site of the Mission Church, which was founded in 1869 by the Redemptionist Fathers, who converted the Dearborn mansion into the first place of worship for the burgeoning German immigrants in the area, many of whom were employed in the extensive breweries along the Stoney Brook.

In a view looking across the street in 1856 from the landscaped forecourt of Boston's Old City Hall on School Street, the temple-fronted Massachusetts Horticultural Society is dwarfed by the marble-facaded Parker House. Harvey Parker opened his famous restaurant and hotel on School Street in 1860, and the impressive Italianate building, identified as Parker's above the entrance, was designed by William Washburn. The now famous Parker House rolls and Boston cream pie were first served to Bostonians at Parker's. The present Parker House Hotel, the oldest continuously operating hotel in America, was designed by G. Henri Desmond and built in 1927. On the right, at the corner of Tremont and School Streets, can be seen a corner of King's Chapel, which was designed by English architect Peter Harrison (1716–1785) and built in 1749.

Harvey Drury Parker (1805–1884) was an entrepreneur who parlayed his restaurant experience into what was, even during his lifetime, a Boston institution. A native of Maine, Parker began a career in food service when he purchased the restaurant of John E. Hunt on Court Square in Boston in 1832. In 1854, he was sufficiently successful to commission a new restaurant and hotel to be built on School Street, adjacent to the Massachusetts Horticultural Society. The society's building was later purchased by Parker in 1860, after which an addition to the hotel was built. A self-made but benevolent man, he was eulogized after his death as "one of the best known of all of the long line of famous American landlords, a genial host, a staunch friend, a worthy citizen, and a benevolent and charitable man." Today, the Parker House still commands the corner of Tremont and School Streets and dispenses the same hospitality as its founder.

The granite building adjacent to the King's Chapel Burying Ground was built by the Provident Institution for Savings, after which it became the headquarters (with the first floor rented to the Suffolk Savings Bank) of the Massachusetts Historical Society from 1833 until they built their headquarters on Boylston Street in the Back Bay Fens. On the left is the Boston Museum, a theater designed by J.H. Hammatt Billings with a four-story granite facade, three stories of gas jets with globes, and an interior that was considered "one of the most elegant theatres in the city in appearance, decoration, and furnishings."

Daniel Bowen (1760–1856) was the proprietor of the Columbian Museum, which from 1806 to 1811 was located on Tremont Street in a building adjacent to the King's Chapel Burying Ground. Here, he is depicted in 1819 by the artist Joseph Kyle. Bowen had become an entrepreneur, partner of silhouettist William M.S. Doyle, and an artist, with a home in Boston and a summerhouse on Bowen's Hill in Brighton. He taught his nephew Abel Bowen the skill of woodcutting, and he, in turn, made the first woodcuts in America, which were used to illustrate Alvah Snow's *History of Boston*. The unique and widespread collections of the museum were eventually purchased in 1841 by Moses Kimball, who opened the Boston Museum and Gallery of Fine Arts at the corner of Tremont and Bromfield Street. It later became Frederick Gleason's office, where *Gleason's Pictorial Drawing Room Companion* was published.

The Tremont House, designed by Isaiah Rogers (1800–1869), was built in 1829 at the corner of Tremont and Beacon Streets, adjacent to the Old Granary Burying Ground, for owners Messrs. Elliot, Belknap, and Upham. Rogers, although a carpenter and self-taught architect, was to parlay his experience in designing the Tremont House into a nationwide architectural practice for hotels, among which were the Astor House in New York, the Bangor House in Bangor, Maine, and Exchange Hotel in Richmond, Virginia. The Tremont House was an impressive building with a granite facade and four bold Doric columns screening the entrance. It had "always been a first-class hotel, and has had a reputation for solid comfort and quiet elegance in its conduct [and the] efficient management of the house early attained a national reputation." The Tremont House was the most elegant and commodious hotel in Boston in the mid-19th century and had many notable guests, among them Charles Dickens, who described his stay at the hotel as having "more galleries, colonnades, piazzas, and passages than I can remember, or the reader would believe."

In a c.1870 winter view looking north from the corner of Park and Tremont Streets, the corner of the Park Street Church can be seen on the left, with the Studio Buildings and the Massachusetts Horticultural Society on the right. The Horticultural Society had outgrown its first headquarters on School Street and sold the building to Harvey Parker, who built an extension to his hotel. The new building of the society was built on Tremont Street between Bromfield Street and Montgomery Place and faced the Old Granary Burying Ground.

The Massachusetts Horticultural Society's building was designed by Gridley J. Fox Bryant and built in 1864. An impressive building of Concord white granite, it had Doric columns on the first floor, Ionic columns on the second floor, and Corinthian columns on the third floor. Three life-sized statues sculpted by Martin Milmore ornamented the facade—a larger statue of Circes surmounting the parapet and smaller statues of Flora and Pomona on either corner of the facade. On the right are the Studio Buildings, which were artists' space throughout the 19th century and had the much desired western light exposure, which was undeterred by the openness of the Boston Common.

The interior of the gallery of the Massachusetts Horticultural Society had an exhibition in 1869 that was attended by both adults and children. The cramped conditions of the building on School Street had led to tents being erected on the Boston Common, but this commodious and well-lit exhibition hall would serve the weekly displays of society members until the turn of the century, when a larger headquarters and exhibition hall was built in the Back Bay Fens at the corner of Massachusetts and Huntington Avenues.

The former Boston Museum had become Gleason's Publishing Hall, as seen in this photograph from 1862. The elegant granite building had a colonnade of six monumental Corinthian columns on the facade, and it was here Frederick Gleason's well-read weekly newspaper, *Gleason's Pictorial Drawing Room Companion*, was published. On the left can be seen the Tremont Temple. With two stories of heavily arched windows, it was the place of worship for the Union Temple Church and the New England headquarters of the Baptist church. The Tremont Temple had originally held services in the former Tremont Theatre, but this building was designed by William Washburn and built in 1853. On the far left is the portico of King's Chapel, which was designed by Charles Bulfinch and added to the Peter Harrison–designed granite church in 1789 in anticipation of Pres. George Washington's visit to Boston.

A large crowd gathers on Court Street between Tremont and Washington Streets in 1856 to watch a parade from window, rooftop, and sidewalk. The parade was in celebration of the 150th anniversary of the birth of Benjamin Franklin (1706–1790)—a native-born son who rose from obscurity as a printer to a leader of the new republic, as well as a patriot and statesman. The parade wound its way through the streets of the city to city hall on School Street, where the statue of Franklin, sculpted by Richard Saltonstall Greenough, was unveiled and dedicated. Franklin bequeathed a generous legacy to Boston that was prudently invested for 100 years and eventually used to establish the Franklin Institute in Boston's South End. It was also used to purchase large tracts of land that became known as Franklin Park and Franklin Field. In the center distance can be seen the Old State House, with American flags strung across Court Street.

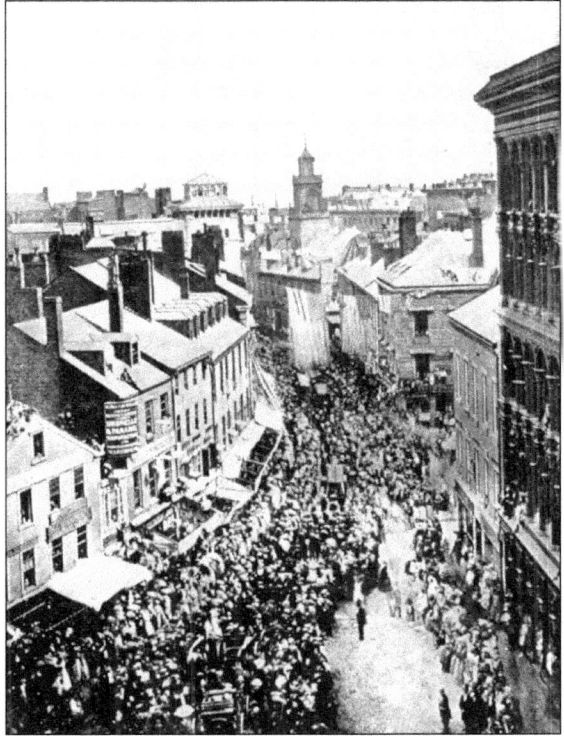

At the time this c. 1870 photograph of State Street was taken, the street was still dominated by the Old State House (center), but it had become the center of the banking and finance of the city after the Civil War. The Ames Building towered over the relic of Boston's Colonial past.

Through days of sorrow and mirth, through days of death and days of birth, Through every swift vicissitude of changeful time, unchanged it has stood.

—Henry Wadsworth Longfellow

41

The Old State House had been covered with advertising signs by the mid-19th century. It had been remodeled by Isaiah Rogers in 1830 with a porch added to the east facade when the building was used as city hall. In 1865, when the new city hall on School Street was completed, the building was leased for commercial purposes, with many of the businesses hanging advertising signs on the exterior, among them the United States Telegraph Company, Reed & Brother Fire & Life Insurance, North American Fire Insurance, and Smith & Company Clothing Warerooms. Eventually, after such an ignoble use of the historic building, it was saved by William H. Whittemore (then Boston city registrar and first president of the newly founded Bostonian Society), who leased the building for a museum. The Old State House was restored by city architect George A. Clough in 1881 and is still the headquarters of the Bostonian Society.

In this *c.* 1885 view looking down State Street from the Old State House, the granite-facaded Union Block can be seen on the left, and Hovey's is on the right at the corner of Devonshire Street. The Union Block replaced the former Royal Custom House and, when it was built in 1810, was among the first buildings in Boston to be built of granite. This was the starting point in 1772 for the first regular stagecoach to New York City.

The *Daily Advertiser* was located on the site of Benjamin Franklin's printing shop on Court Street opposite Court Square. The four-story granite building had a fanciful dormered mansard roof and was demolished in 1883 for the Fay Building, which became the site of the Old Colony Trust Company in 1908.

Washington Street, opposite Milk Street, was built up with commercial buildings, as seen in this photograph from 1870. St. Joachim Bazaar, seen on the left, was at 167 Washington Street and offered fancy goods and clothing. Next door, in an impressive building, was Benjamin French & Company, importers and manufacturers of photographic materials. On the right can be seen a corner of the Old South Meeting House, and horse-drawn streetcars can be seen approaching from the area of Washington Street between School and State Streets.

Winter Street, which extends from Tremont to Washington Streets, is shown in the winter of 1871, looking west toward the Boston Common. On the right, the men stand in front of the entrance to the Boston Music Hall, with a gas lantern identifying it directly above. (Courtesy William Varrell.)

Milk Street, shown in a view looking east from Washington Street, had the Old South Meeting House (left) and the Boys' Clothing House (right), which offered clothing both wholesale and retail. These four- and five-story commercial buildings created a densely built-up district that offered numerous stores for the shopper.

Boston City Hall was built between 1862 and 1865 on School Street, between King's Chapel and the Niles Building. Designed by J. Gridley Fox Bryant and Arthur Gilman, it was an impressive building with a Louvre-inspired dome surmounted by a winged eagle. It was built in the Italian Renaissance style of architecture "as modified and elaborated by modern French architects" and is as impressive today as when it was built almost a century and a half ago. White Concord granite was used on its facade, but the sides facing Court Square and City Hall Avenue are faced with Chelmsford granite that was prudently and economically salvaged from the old courthouse, which previously stood on the site. In front of what is now referred to as Old City Hall are statues of Benjamin Franklin (1706–1790), sculpted by Richard Saltonstall Greenough, and Josiah Quincy (1772–1864), sculpted by Thomas Bell.

The Niles Block was a step-gabled end facade building on School Street that was located adjacent to Boston City Hall.

A view of Water Street, looking from Congress Street toward Washington Street in the mid-1860s, shows the street lined with brick and granite commercial buildings with a plethora of advertising signs that created a vibrant and densely built-up district. The uniform granite facade on the right is the Simmons Block, where owner T.A. Simmons sold ready-made clothing and furnishing goods. It was designed by Carl Fehmer, and the buildings on the left were demolished in 1869 to make way for the new post office and subtreasury that was built on Congress Street between Milk and Water Streets. The cobblestone streets and the well-worn granite slab walkways create an interesting aspect to the dressed granite used for many of the buildings.

This five-story building was designed by Nathaniel J. Bradlee and William T. Winslow and built in 1873 at the corner of Franklin and Devonshire Streets. The building was indicative of the size and scale of buildings built in the financial district following the Great Boston Fire of 1872.

State Street, shown in an 1865 view looking east from Congress Street, had a more domestic scale than it does today. On the left can be seen the Union Block with the Suffolk Bank. On the right is the temple-fronted Merchants Exchange.

Washington Street, or that area between State and School Streets referred to as Cornhill, was completely commercial by the time of the Civil War. The advertising signage in this section of the street runs the gamut from poetical and mathematical instruments, printing and engraving, and drugs and medicine to shoes, clothing, and dye houses—truly an all-service area.

The corner of Tremont and Winter Streets opposite the Boston Common had been a commercial district since the 1850s. The former rowhouse on the corner, 130 Tremont Street, had become Mrs. L.N. Mason & Company, which offered French millinery for fashion-conscious Bostonians. It was also a custom shirt shop and laundry. Notice the fanciful second-floor oriel window with its dome-like finial that has a window display for curious onlookers. This corner building was eventually demolished, and a brownstone commercial block was designed by John A. Fox (1835–1920) and built in 1883. In the foreground is part of the cast-iron railing and balusters surrounding Boston Common.

The Second Universalist Church was built in 1817 on School Street near the corner of Province Street. The congregation later remodeled the building in 1851 with a corner-quoined Italianate facade that had shops on either side of the front entrance. Samuel Gerrish, tailor, was on the right and Hervy & Masters, merchant tailors, were on the left. The Boston Five Cents Savings Bank was founded in 1854 in this building and was located here for well over a century, until it built a larger headquarters on School Street between Washington and Province Streets.

Officers and clerks of the Boston Five Cents Savings Bank in 1866 included, from left to right, the following: (seated) George Tothill, William E. Titcomb, Alonzo H. Evans, Pres. Paul Adams, Curtis C. Nichols, and James Foster; (standing) Irving A. Evans, Don A. Clay, Elmer C. Gordon, George F. Foster, and Rogers I. Barstow.

The Wesleyan Association Building was designed by J.H. Hammatt Billings and his brother Joseph Billings and built in 1870 at 36 Bromfield. A four-story granite building that served as the headquarters of the Methodist church in Boston, it was later a part of Boston University. The gas lantern projecting from the facade identifies the entrance to Wesleyan Hall. On the right is the Bromfield Street Church, and on the left is a row of granite-facaded Greek Revival buildings at 30-36 Bromfield Street that were built in 1848 with Doric pilasters, which flanked the windows and supported the cornice.

The Aquarial Gardens

THE LEARNED SEALS

This intensely interesting Exhibition has lately received very important additions, namely,

A LIVING PELICAN, from the Gulf of Mexico.

That rare and interesting animal, the AGOUTI, from Para.

A pair of live OPOSSUMS, from Georgia.

A Magnificent living specimen of the AMERICAN GOLDEN EAGLE.

A pair of splendid AMERICAN HORNED OWLS, &c. &c.

The MARBLED SEALS astonish and delight every one by their wonderful intelligence

The LIVING ALLIGATOR and all the great variety of Fish in the Glass Tank

Also to be seen, the DEN OF SERPENTS, which contains within its transparent

Aquarial Gardens, 21 Bromfield Street.

CUTTING & BUTLER, Proprietors.

The Aquarial Gardens was located at 21 Bromfield Street, where curious Bostonians were drawn to see the learned seals, as well as an assortment of curiosities, such as a living pelican, the agouti from Parsa, a pair of opossums from Georgia, an American golden eagle, and an American horned owl. The Aquarial Gardens, operated by Cutting and Butler, had numerous animal shows to entertain the curious, as well as large fish tanks of marine life that were the precursor to our present Boston Aquarium.

The Boston Museum was built in 1846 on Tremont Street near the corner of Court Street. Designed by J.H. Hammatt Billings, the theater was referred to as a museum in deference to the delicate sensibilities of Bostonians who still harbored reservations about theatrical performances and their attendance. The theater itself was called the Lecture Hall. On the left is the S.S. Pierce & Company, founded in 1831 by Silas Stillman Pierce. It was replaced by the Hemenway Building, which was designed by Nathaniel J. Bradlee and built of red brick and hewn brownstone in 1880. The Boston Museum was demolished in 1903, and on its site was built the Kimball Building at 18-22 Tremont Street, named for Moses Kimball, the proprietor of the old Boston Museum.

The imposing interior foyer of the Boston Museum had monumental Corinthian columns supporting a barrel-vaulted ceiling with the enormous canvas *Washington Crossing the Delaware*, by Thomas Sully, on the far wall. The museum was entered by a granite facade with large gas jets on each story. The theater had curiosities and exhibits that allowed ladies and those not in the habit of attending theaters to justify their attendance as an intellectual pursuit and not that of entertainment. The Grand Hall of Cabinets, seen in the accompanying photograph, and its statuary and paintings were once the wonder and delight of visitors. Among the more unique exhibits was the Feejee mermaid, a curiosity coveted by the great showman P.T. Barnum.

The Cathedral Building was designed by Gridley J. Fox Bryant (1816–1899) and built on the former site of the Cathedral of the Holy Cross. An impressive five-story commercial block, it was owned by Patrick Donahue, editor of the *Boston Pilot*, the oldest Catholic newspaper in New England, which was published in the building. Tenants of the building included Whitten, Burdett & Young, Keating Lang & Company, and Barnes, Merriam & Company, all leading ready-made clothing stores.

Franklin Street was rebuilt in 1858 with granite-facaded commercial buildings designed by Gridley J. Fox Bryant that replaced the Tontine Crescent. The new buildings retained the gently curving streetscape laid out by Charles Bulfinch in the 1790s, with the commercial facades following the once elegant neoclassical residential facades. The remnant of the center green was a lone tree that stood in the middle of the street with an embankment to protect it from wagons and carts. (Courtesy William Varrell.)

Three

THE GREAT BOSTON FIRE
OF 1872

The Great Boston Fire of 1872 destroyed 40 acres of downtown Boston, an area bounded by Washington, Avon, and Milk Streets and the waterfront. The fire destroyed almost 800 buildings, numerous churches, and millions of dollars of merchandise, but it also swept away old Boston, enabling architects to rebuild the city as its appellation "Hub of the Universe" was to give credence.

The old South End had once been the place of fashionable residences, which, by the time of the Civil War, had given way to commercial blocks and business concerns. The elegant mansions had been replaced by four- and five-story commercial blocks with fashionable mansard roofs. The effect was one of progress, and most Bostonians perceived it as the culmination of a postwar economic boom that brought great benefits to the city. However, the growth was often haphazard and ill planned, with buildings built without concern for water pressure, narrow streets, safety, or building materials. The fire, which began in Leman Klous' Hoop Skirt Factory at the corner of Summer and Kingston Streets, was to have a head start by the fact that most city horses were experiencing an epizootic, whereby they were under the weather when the fire began.

The Great Boston Fire, a story retold by many, was not just a financial loss to the city and its business community, but a moral one. Rev. Dr. Webb of the Shawmut Church of Boston took a hard-line view of the devastation and preached the Sunday following the fire, saying, "We are under a government which embraces the minutes events. Some natural law is violated and the penalty follows. Combustible roofs, like the grass of the prairie, fed the fire as it flew. Had it not burned into our souls that only men wise in foresight, quick to discern, prompt in act, capable of leading in the hour of danger, should be entrusted with the city's affairs? The penalty for imperfect work or design, as in a ship of a safe, is disaster. This calamity is the work of Providence; but he who lets matters rest there without investigation is a fool."

By Heaven! it is a splendid sight to see, for one who hath no friend, no brother, there.

The Burnt District of Boston was a 40-acre area bounded by Washington, Avon, and Milk Streets and the waterfront. By the time the fire had been extinguished, it had destroyed almost 800 commercial buildings, in an area that, although once a fashionable place of residence, had become almost wholly commercial and the pride of Boston. Commercial blocks of four- and five-story granite, brick, and marble buildings with the then popular and fashionable mansard roof, proved to be a great reason the fire spread as the roofs fed the fire as it flew. The devastation was tremendous and seemingly all inclusive.

In a popular Currier & Ives print entitled *Boston in Flames*, the Great Boston Fire was depicted in a dramatic effect with the fire engulfing the Summer Street area of the city with excursion boats, ships, and passenger ferries anchored just off the coast and dangerously filled with curious onlookers. The dome of the Massachusetts State House surmounts Beacon Hill in the center. The fire burned for four days and destroyed the center of the cotton, wool, and retail district of the city, destroying property to the 1872 value of $100 million. As described by Col. William Conwell in his book *The History of the Great Fire,* "Yet the fire paused not, but ran riot with demonical glee, as it scorched through the windows, and drove the excited owners away from their own doors."

The Cathedral Building had only recently been completed in 1871 but was destroyed in a matter of hours by the intensity of the fire. Firefighters valiantly tried to play water on the fire, but the water pressure was too weak for the streams to reach the burning roof. These roofs were constructed of wood trusses, over which was laid a slate and copper roof that literally acted as a vacuum for the flames, which burst through the top of the building at lightning speed. The *Pilot,* New England's leading Catholic newspaper, founded in 1836, was printed here by Patrick Donahue, who was ruined by the fire's destruction, which amounted to a loss of over $300,000. Donahue's resilience was tremendous, as he continued the *Pilot* and, in 1878, founded the immensely popular periodical *Donahue's Monthly Magazine.*

The cover of this sheet music was entitled "Homeless Tonight, or Boston in Ashes" and was dedicated to William F. Chase of the Suffolk Hose Company No. 5 in Boston. The dramatic full-color chromolithograph was printed by J.H. Bufford's Sons and shows two shoeless girls clinging to one another as they escape the fire engulfing Summer Street, with Trinity Church in the background. The sheet music had words and music by local songwriter C.A. White and was sold to the public so one could re-create the excitement of the night at home on the family piano. (Courtesy Boston Athenaeum collection.)

The devastation of the Burnt District in the aftermath of the fire was tremendous, and many businesses and merchants were ruined. Although most buildings were destroyed by fire, such as Trinity Church on the right, others had been destroyed by causes other than by fire. On the left are C.F. Hovey & Company and R.H. Stearns & Company on Summer Street, which surprisingly survived the fire. Farther down the street, Shreve, Crump & Low had also survived the fire but was destroyed on Sunday night, November 10, by a gas main explosion, which ruptured and blew off the facade of the building. Winter Street can be seen in the center distance and was unaffected by the fire, which ended at Washington Street.

To protect property and to dissuade the curious public, the Claflin Guards of the Massachusetts Militia were called out by the governor to restore order. Here, at the corner of Kilby and Water Streets, Capt. W.B. Sears (center) and the members of the Claflin Guards pose in formation on Liberty Square in front of the shells of former commercial blocks for a photograph on November 12, 1872.

The tower of Trinity Church stands as a stark reminder of its former importance on Summer Street. The crenellated tower and its flanking sides show the ravages of fire and the fact that the interior was completely gutted. The door openings have been sheathed in wood planking to exclude the curious. Eventually, a wood-plank canopy would be erected over the front of the church to protect passersby of falling debris from the tower. A fireman stands in the right foreground, talking with workmen clearing the fallen debris.

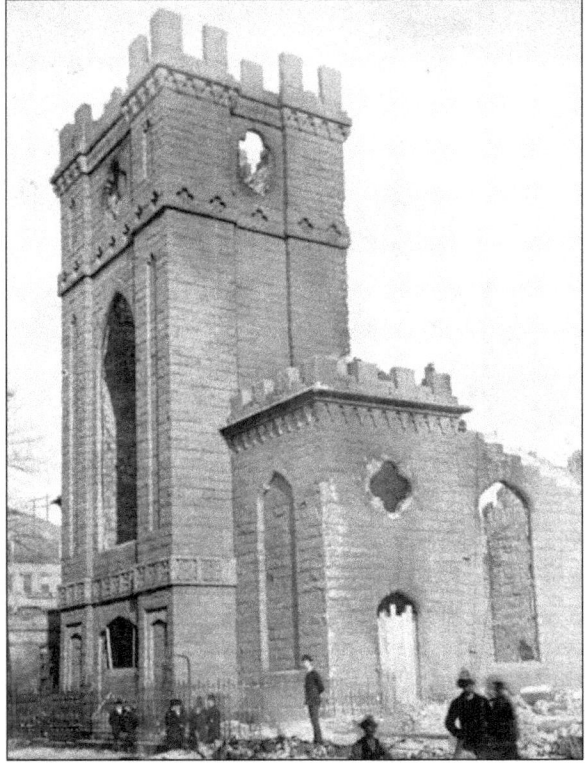

The interior of Trinity Church shows the floor having been burnt away with the crypts in the basement of the church lying open. As early as 1829, when the church was completed, crypts were sold to parishioners for the future burial of family and friends. Here, the cast-iron crypt doors are open. The coffins were promptly removed for reburial in surrounding cemeteries, such as Mount Auburn Cemetery in Cambridge and Forest Hills, Cedar Grove, and Mount Hope Cemeteries in Boston. Today, Filene's Basement is located in the former crypts of Trinity Church. Notice the lancet-shaped openings on the west wall, which had all traces of the memorial windows destroyed in the fire.

57

Businessmen pose for a group photograph, some sitting on chunks of imploded granite, with the picturesque ruins of former commercial blocks on Pearl Street creating a dramatic and macabre backdrop. On the right is a remnant of an entrance to a lost building with the names of businesses still visible. These businesses were A.A. Gilmore & Company, J.D. Pike & Company, and J.D. Warren & Company, and the men may have been associated with these businesses.

A member of the Claflin Guards of the Massachusetts Militia stands in front of the once elegant Corinthian-columned, triarched facade of Macullar, Williams & Parker on Washington Street between Franklin and Summer Streets. The company, completely destroyed in a matter of hours, had moved its office to 15 Tremont Street, as the sign behind the guard states. The ready-made clothing operation would be reestablished in a matter of weeks, and the business would eventually have a large warehouse and factory that employed over 400 workers. This poignant photograph captures the devastation, which is artistically framed by the remnants that stand as if to shield the onlooker from the true devastation that had occurred.

A firefighter stands with a man in front of ruins on Summer Street. These firemen, many of whom were on duty for days after the fire and slept at the Old South Meeting House, continued to spray the smoldering ruins with water from the miles of canvas fire hoses that littered the streets of the Burnt District for weeks after the fire was over. The grotesque remains of the once fashionable granite and brownstone commercial blocks rise like fingers pointing to the heavens from the rubble-strewn area.

"The Cataract," or Steamer No. 10, was assigned to the Mount Vernon Street Firehouse on the flat of Beacon Hill, but it was to remain near Post Office Square for weeks after the fire to preclude any flareups that needed to be extinguished. Here, on Devonshire Street, a group of men poses for a photographer near the steamer with the post office and subtreasury seen on the left. A fireman, on the right, hoses down the smoldering debris on Post Office Square, which was described as "a vast city of ruins, the limit of which could at no point be seen, still smoking and steaming violently from the shock that had caused its fearful overthrow."

A group of men stands on piles of debris on Franklin Street with the uncompleted subtreasury and post office on Congress Street seen in the distance. The post office and subtreasury, a massive building of Cape Ann granite, was on Congress Street between Milk and Water Streets facing Post Office Square and was the dominant building in that area of the financial district. Notice the sign that translates to "Oh, I see" from pictorial language, for the business once located at this site had moved its office to a new location in the city.

With the post office and subtreasury as a backdrop, these men stand on either side of piles of clothing that had been thrown from burning buildings and represented part of the extensive debris that had to be cleaned up. The clothing seen here had once been part of the stock of Freeland, Harding, and Richardson's store on Devonshire Street, one of many ready-made clothing warehouses and stores located in the area, and almost every one of which was destroyed.

Congress Street, seen in a view looking east from Water Street, has shells of former buildings as a backdrop to this photograph. On the right is the small wood shed of Charles Woodbery & Son, a mason who literally set up shop, so to speak, in the midst of the ruins and proffered his services in the massive cleanup project.

This flatiron building was at the junction of High and Summer Streets. The fire had destroyed adjoining buildings as "the great heat caused strong currents of air, and caused the winds to whistle about the corners and alleys as fierce and cold as January." On the left can be seen mounds of debris that had been cleared from Summer Street, seen in the center, and eventually had to be removed in the massive rebuilding of the Burnt District.

The Old South Meeting House, an important and historic spot that was beloved by Bostonians for its Revolutionary War associations, was saved through the valiant efforts of numerous citizens who spread wet blankets on the roof, and more importantly, the fact that "the Kearsage," a pumper engine from Portsmouth, New Hampshire, remained throughout the night, spraying water on the roof and spire to preclude its destruction by the encroaching fire. Here, the shadows cast by the setting sun shine through the destroyed buildings and are eerily reflected on the walls of Old South and create a macabre image of the extent of what was lost and what was saved.

The massive cleanup of the Burnt District was organized by the city within a few days of the fire, and most of the streets were cleared of debris for ease of movement within days. Here, temporary wood sheds were erected in the area of Purchase Street for workers to eat and sleep during the cleanup project, which would take months and was under the direction of new city architect George Clough. On the right can be seen the dome of the Massachusetts State House, flanked by the spires of the Park Street Church and the Old South Meeting House, recognizable landmarks in a field of debris.

Four

BANKING AND FINANCE

Boston has been the banking and finance capital of New England, with State Street in Boston's financial district being the center of this activity. It was said of State Street in 1893, "Here are now to be found some of the finest specimens of modern architecture; and no business section of any of our American cities presents more solid and attractive features than this one does."

State Street began to change rapidly after the Civil War, from the four- and five-story brick and granite buildings of the early 19th century to the Richards Building (erected in 1867), the earliest surviving example of a cast-iron structure in the financial district. The capitalists of the city showed great and decisive "boldness and energy in the furthering of enterprises in distant sections of the country than they have in the inauguration and development of undertakings in the New England district."

By the 1870s, after the massive devastation of Boston's financial district by the Great Boston Fire of 1872, tremendous building took place in Boston and the area of State Street. Surrounding streets began to be developed with taller, grander buildings that became the pride of the city. In the last quarter of the 19th century, more than 100 banks, financial institutions, and trust companies were offering their services to the general public, businesses, and larger concerns. With new buildings, a broader outlook in finance, and a burgeoning population base that had increased tremendously through immigration and the annexation of the surrounding cities of Roxbury and Charlestown and the towns of Dorchester, West Roxbury (which included Jamaica Plain and Roslindale), Brighton, and Hyde Park, the numerous banking and financial concerns competed against one another for the private and corporate investors.

The financial district had become the pride of a municipal government that saw its direction of the building of the area, through a city architect appointed between 1873 and 1905, as among its greatest accomplishments.

A view looking north on Summer Street from Church Green in 1890 shows the street completely rebuilt after everything in the vicinity was destroyed by the Great Boston Fire of 1872. In 1873, the first city architect was George A. Clough, who began rebuilding the city in a systematic approach with high-rise buildings set along the cleared and widened streets. On the left is the Church Green Building at the corner of Bedford and Summer Streets, designed by Jonathan Preston. At the corner of Summer and Devonshire Streets, on the right, is the Manufacturers National Bank, which was built in 1873. In the distance can be seen the spire of the Park Street Church, rising above the buildings on Washington Street at Winter Street, today referred to as Downtown Crossing.

The Equitable Life Assurance Society of New York Building, designed by Arthur Gilman (1821–1882), was built in 1875 on Milk Street near Post Office Square. Gilman was a famous wit and able architect who designed the Equitable Building. The building, "whose details showed a more sophisticated taste than those of the city hall," was built on School Street in Boston.

The new building of the *Boston Herald*, which was founded in 1846, was located at Cornhill. A granite five-story building in the French Renaissance style of architecture, it was built in 1878 with an interesting roof with a projecting dormer and set between earlier granite Greek Revival buildings that had once created a somewhat uniform streetscape height. The *Boston Herald* was printed on six Bullock presses, each press capable of printing 21,500 newspapers an hour. At 1¢ per copy, it was a widely read newspaper and had several morning and evening editions.

A part of Washington Street was called Newspaper Row when the *Boston Herald*, the *Boston Transcript*, and the *Boston Globe* were located there in the early years of the 20th century. Here, businessmen, newspapermen, a paperboy, and shoppers throng the street near Court Street c. 1905.

This 1885 view of State Street looks east from the Old State House and shows members of the 1st Regiment of the Massachusetts Volunteer Militia stopped on their march up State Street before departing by train from South Station. Their next stop was New York, where they participated in the funeral of Ulysses S. Grant, former U.S. president. This regiment included a gallant colonel, Austin C. Wellington, who followed Grant in many hard-fought battles during the Civil War. State Street had a combination of 19th-century buildings, including the tri-arched granite Union Block on the left, and the Ionic colonnaded Suffolk Bank farther down the street. On the right is the Merchants Exchange, which was designed by Isaiah Rogers and built in 1842. On the far right is a corner of the Tremont National Bank, which faces Congress Street, and a tea-delivery wagon trying to move through the densely packed spectators. (Courtesy private collection.)

The Fiske Building, seen from Merchants Row, was an impressive structure designed by Peabody & Stearns and built in 1888. The rough-hewn granite was often referred to as Boston Granite style. Here, the architects created a vertical high rise with banks of windows on the facade. The windows led to the segmental arches flanking a dormer with slate roofs above. Today, the site of the Fiske Building is home to the Graham Gund Associates. Skidmore, Owings, & Merrill designed 75 State Street, which was built in 1988.

In a view looking west on State Street, the Fiske Building can be seen on the left. The Exchange Building, at 53 State Street, was designed by Peabody & Stearns and built in 1891. Both the Fiske Building and the State Street Exchange transformed the street from an important business street to the banking and finance center of New England. This area was once referred to as the Exchange in imitation of the London section where businessmen of the city met daily to transact business.

The State Street Exchange Building was designed by the noted architectural firm of Peabody & Stearns. It was built on the site of the former Greek Revival Merchants Exchange on State Street between Kilby and Congress Streets. It was a massive, fireproof office building and served as the first home of the Boston Stock Exchange. On the left can be seen a corner of the Harvey Fisk & Sons Building with its corner roof clock. The facade of the State Street Exchange survives today thanks to a determined group of preservationists. It serves as a base of Exchange Place, a sleek glass office tower designed by the WZMH Group and built in 1981.

The interior of the Boston Stock Exchange, in the Exchange Building, had an impressive room lighted by large arched windows and an enormous glass dome above the trading stations. Membership in the exchange has always been limited according to the bylaws, and regular calls were made at 10:30 a.m. and 1:30 p.m. during the business day.

This view looking west on State Street from India Street shows the financial district of Boston. This was well established by the 1880s with prominent banking houses, investment and bond dealers, and others located in the new buildings in the area.

A streetcar that connected East Cambridge and South Boston crosses Congress Street on Flag Day in this view looking east from the Old State House in 1914. The American flag flies from the high-rise buildings in the area. The old Union Block still survives on the left (now the site of 60 State Street) with the Fiske Building at 75 State Street. The Merchants Exchange and the Tremont National Bank are on the right.

The Boston Chamber of Commerce Building was designed by Shepley, Rutan, and Coolidge, successors of H.H. Richardson, and was built in 1892. The modified Gothic building with massive piers and arches was built of rough-hewn pink Worcester granite at the junction of India Street and Central Wharf. It has a gabled conical roof that sits like a crown on the top of the building and is surrounded by a tiara-like pinnacled crenellation, which surrounds its turreted roof. The building had trade rooms, reading rooms, committee rooms, and offices. Today, it is referred to as the Grain Exchange and has numerous private offices.

The entrance to the Boston Chamber of Commerce Building was a Romanesque arch set within a pediment with colonettes supporting the base. By 1890, the area around the Boston Custom House had been completely infilled. Boston Harbor did not come up to the east steps of the custom house any longer, and sailing ships stopped docking there. The area had become a densely built commercial district, and the Boston Chamber of Commerce Building was a prominent landmark.

Boston's financial district was never more impressive or imposing than in this photograph from 1916. The recently completed custom house tower was designed by the noted architectural firm of Peabody & Stearns and built in 1915 above the original Greek Revival structure, which was completed in 1849. The custom house was an important Federal building and was located just south of State Street. Today, it is the Marriott Custom House. On the left can be seen the Boston Board of Trade Building, and on the right is the Boston Chamber of Commerce Building (the Grain Exchange), which was said in the early 20th century to be one of the "most aggressive commercial bodies in any American city."

Boston's city hall was built in 1865 on School Street. By 1910, it was set in a densely built-up area that included City Hall Avenue on the right, an alleyway that led to Court Square and Court Street, as well as the historic King's Chapel and its burying ground on the left. The two statues in the forecourt of the city hall are Benjamin Franklin (1706–1790) on the left, sculpted by Richard Saltonstall Geenough, and on the right is Josiah Quincy (1772–1864), which was sculpted by Thomas Ball. Rising above King's Chapel is the Albion Building, which is the home of the Houghton & Dutton Department Store, located on the corner of Tremont and Beacon Streets. The building is now the site of 1 Beacon Street.

The Ames Building was designed by the Boston architectural firm of Shepley, Rutan & Coolidge, successors to H.H. Richardson, and was built in 1889 at the corner of Court and Washington Streets. When it was built, the Ames Building was the tallest building on the East Coast. It had a series of Romanesque arches that heightened its verticality. The building is capped by a robust overhanging cornice with stone bracketing and windows between them. In the foreground is the Ruskinian Gothic Sears Building, which had the first elevator in the city of Boston.

In a view looking west on School Street, the forecourt of Old City Hall can be seen on the right with a corner of King's Chapel and the top of the Albion Building rising above. On the left is the Parker House, a historic institution in the city and the oldest continuously operating hotel in the United States.

The Tremont Building was designed by Winslow & Wetherall and built in 1895 at the corner of Tremont and Beacon Streets, adjacent to the Old Granary Burying Ground. Built on the site of the Tremont House, Boston's first luxury hotel, it was considered at the turn of the century to be "one of the biggest and best equipped office buildings in Boston, is well lighted, heated, ventilated, and thoroughly modern in every respect."

The Shawmut National Bank Building is under construction in 1906 in the financial district. Designed by Winslow & Bigelow and built by L.P. Soule & Son Company, this impressive granite building was built on Water Street from Devonshire to Congress Streets. It had an entrance of four bold Doric columns supporting an office floor and was flanked by projecting wings with a recessed center block. At the time of its opening, it was said to be "unsurpassed by any office building in New England," and a "fitting and worthy monument to one of America's strongest and most ably managed financial institutions."

The Boston Board of Trade Building was designed by Winslow & Bigelow and built in 1901 on State Street between Broad and India Streets. On the left can be seen a corner of the Boston Custom House, designed by Ammi Burnham Young and built of Quincy granite between 1837 and 1849.

The headquarters of the John Hancock Mutual Life Insurance Company was designed by Winslow & Bigelow and was built at the corner of Federal and Franklin Streets. Established in 1853 and incorporated in 1862, the company was said to have had "an uninterrupted record of annual dividends" since its founding. It had long been located in Boston's financial district and shared its headquarters with the Eliot National Bank. In the 1920s, the company built a new office building in the Back Bay.

The Boston Chamber of Commerce Building was erected in 1924 at 80 Federal Street. The chamber of commerce was first established in 1795 at a time of great activity for Boston merchants. It went into abeyance until 1836, when it was revived by William Sturgis, who served as its new president. However, it was in 1885 that the modern Boston Chamber of Commerce came into existence with the merger of the Commercial and Produce Exchanges. Their objective was "to promote just and equitable principles of trade; to establish and maintain uniformity in commercial usages; to correct any abuses which may exist; to acquire, preserve, and disseminate valuable information . . . and generally, to advance the interests of trade and commerce in the city of Boston," all of which was sanctioned by the state legislature.

The Boston City Hall annex was designed by Edward T.P. Graham and built in 1912 on Court Street with an impressive facade. The steel-framed building has four fluted monumental engaged Corinthian columns supporting an attic, which were ornamented by four life-sized allegorical female figures sculpted by Roger Noble Burnham and set between the attic windows. Today, this is the headquarters of the Boston School Committee.

The steaming teakettle projects from the Sears block, which is a granite post-and-lintel building of 1848. It has been a Boston landmark since 1874, when it was hung by the Oriental Tea Company. Its capacity is marked on the side as 227 gallons, 2 quarts, 1 pint, and 3 gills—an appropriate question for a Bostonian appearing on *Jeopardy*. The Sears block was renovated in 1969 by Don Stull Associates. In the distance, the impressive facade of the Boston City Hall annex can be seen, now the Boston School Committee Building. Notice that the attic is now devoid of the four allegorical female statues. They were removed *c.* 1950 due to safety concerns.

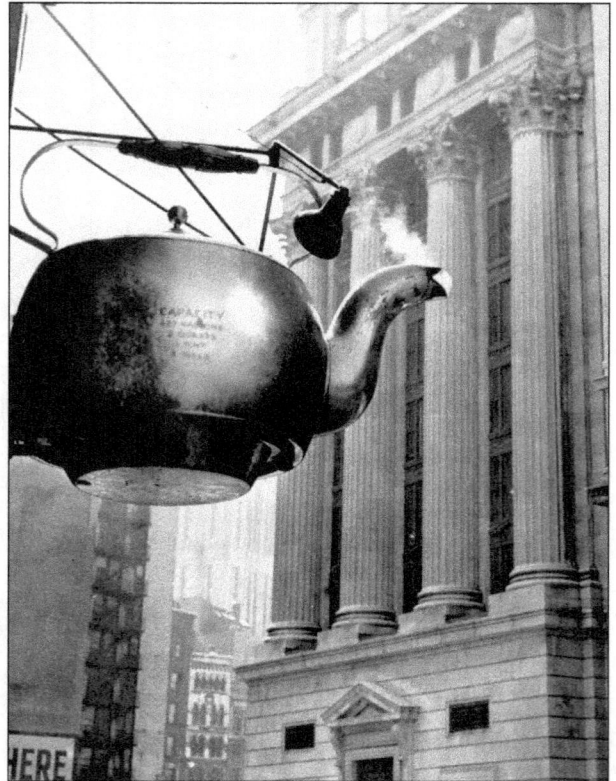

Five

HALLS OF COMMERCE

"The history of the Boston financial institutions is practically identical with that of the steady growth of the city in the confidence of the business public, for the policy of the Boston banks has been such as to make their names synonymous with integrity, intelligence, and solidity." This growth in confidence, and the obvious profits derived from money loans, provided the impetus for the new halls of commerce that were built in Boston's financial district. In the mid-19th century, many banks invested capital in the westward expansion of the railroad. Growth was tremendous, with "ten thousand miles of railroad" tracks having been laid in the West in 1880.

   In the last decade of the 19th century, Boston banks and capitalists had "become more conservative than they were at an earlier period in the country's industrial history, but although they are less venturesome, they are also less expectant of securing high rates of interest, and Boston is now looked upon as the best place in the country at which to promptly obtain money on good security at the very lowest market rates." Granted, capitalists may have become more conservative and cautious in their investment approach, but the buildings they had built in Boston were anything but conservative, with architects who designed many of these "halls of commerce" reading like a *Who's Who* of American architecture. Among these architects and architectural firms were Gridley J. Fox Bryant, William Gibbons Preston, Nathaniel J. Bradlee, Cummings & Sears, Peabody & Stearns, Winslow & Wetherall, Shepley, Rutan & Coolidge, Parker, Thomas & Rice, Henry Field Kellog, R. Clipston Sturgis, and Cram & Ferguson. The area of Boston's financial district is replete with a panoply of architectural styles over the last four decades.

The massive subtreasury and post office was designed by A.A. Mullett, in association with Gridley J. Fox Bryant and Alexander R. Esty, and was built between 1868 and 1875 on Congress Street between Milk and Water Streets. This impressive Cape Ann–granite Renaissance-style building survived the Great Boston Fire of 1872 with only minor damage to its facade. The 200-foot facade was ornamented by two marble groups sculpted by Daniel Chester French (1850–1931) that flanked the mansard roof of the projecting center pavilion. On the left is *Labor* and on the right is *Science*. In the foreground is the Peabody & Stearns–designed memorial to George Thorndike Angell, founder of the Massachusetts Society for the Prevention of Cruelty to Animals (MSPCA) and for whom the Angell Memorial Hospital was named. There is now a park, known as Angell Memorial Park, in the center of Post Office Square, which was designed by Earl Flansburgh and Associates and is a pleasant place to relax on a summer afternoon.

In a view looking up Milk Street from Post Office Square in 1893, a horse-drawn delivery wagon loaded with wooden kegs turns onto Pearl Street. On the right is the Massachusetts Loan and Trust Company, now the site of Le Meridien Hotel. The Equitable Building on Milk Street can be seen in the center distance. On the far left is the dual facade of the New York Mutual Life Insurance Company and the New England Mutual Life Insurance Company, now the site of the Art Deco Telephone Building, which was designed by Cram & Ferguson and built in 1947–1952.

A view looking down Congress Street toward Post Office Square in 1895 shows the area that was once the paper trade in the city. The subtreasury and post office dominates the gently curving streetscape, which is busy with horse-drawn delivery wagons.

Post Office Square was easily accessible from most parts of the city by streetcars. Streetcar No. 1002, which was built in 1900 by Osgood Bradley of Worcester, stops in 1903 for this photograph on its way to Franklin Field in Dorchester from its departure point at North Station. This streetcar would wind itself through the city streets, eventually stopping at South Station, Post Office Square, and Columbia Road in Dorchester and providing passengers with transportation for a nickel. On the right is the New York Mutual Life Insurance Company building, designed by Peabody & Stearns. The Converse Building, at the corner of Milk and Pearl Streets, is in the center. (Courtesy Frank Cheney.)

The south side of Post Office Square was dominated by the impressive Mutual Life Insurance Company of New York on the left and the New England Mutual Life Insurance Company on the right. The Mutual Life Insurance Company of New York building was designed by Peabody & Stearns and built in 1875. The New England Mutual Life Insurance Company building was designed by Nathaniel J. Bradlee and built in 1874.

A detail photograph of the New England Mutual Life Insurance Company, at the corner of Milk and Congress Streets, shows it as an impressive building of white marble with an emblematic bronze group on the mansard roof parapet. Nathaniel J. Bradlee (1829–1888) was a noted architect and principal in the firm of Bradlee, Winslow & Wetherall, which specialized in commercial buildings in the second half of the 19th century. Bradlee's design for this building was as impressive as it was monumental.

The Converse Building was a 10-story steel-frame building of brick and limestone trimmings at the corner of Milk and Pearl Streets in Post Office Square.

The Minot Building, located at the corner of Devonshire and Water Streets, dominates the center of this photograph. On the far left is the flag-draped Lawrence Building, designed by Parker, Thomas and Rice, with the Second National Bank. To its right is the Winthrop Building, and to the right of the photograph can be seen a corner of the subtreasury and post office building, designed by A.A. Mullett. In the distance are the *Boston Advertiser* and the *Boston Globe* buildings, where two of the leading daily newspapers of the early 20th century were published.

Devonshire Street, shown in a view looking from Franklin Street, had become an area of high-rise office buildings by the first decade of the 20th century. On the left is the impressive Boston Safe Deposit and Trust Company Building, now the Boston Stock Exchange, which was designed by the noted architectural firm of Shepley, Rutan & Coolidge and built in 1908–1911.

The Shawmut National Bank was founded in 1836 as a state bank and reorganized in 1865 as a national bank. In 1873, the Howe Building, a Ruskinian Gothic brick and limestone building, was built at the corner of Congress and Water Streets. The bank had its headquarters here, as did the Aetna Insurance Company.

The Manufacturers National Bank was designed by George A. Clough and built in 1873 at the corner of Summer and Devonshire Streets. The Manufacturers National Bank was incorporated in 1873 and merged in 1898 with the Continental National Bank, when the name was changed to the Colonial National Bank. A five-story office building with a partial six story in which a corner clock was placed, it was among the first of the new buildings constructed after the Great Boston Fire of 1872 destroyed this area.

The first-floor offices of the Manufacturers National Bank had tellers behind wire cages, which were as decorative as they were practical. "The Manufacturers National Bank is one of the sturdy landmarks in the path of sound finance, and . . . has ever lent assistance to the full extent of its ability to legitimate enterprise."

The Revere National Bank was incorporated in 1859 and became a national bank in 1865. The banking offices were moved to this Ruskinian Gothic building, which was designed by Peabody & Stearns in 1873 at 100 Franklin Street. The bank was absorbed by the National Shawmut Bank in 1898. On the right are Devonshire Street and the eventual site of the Shawmut Bank of Boston, which was designed by the Architects Collaborative and built in 1975.

Harvey Fisk & Sons were dealers in government bonds, first-class bonds, and investment securities. The company was located at 75 State Street in a four-story building that had a cantilevered corner with a recessed entrance and a corner clock at the roofline. The Fiske Building, which was commissioned by J.N. Fiske, was designed by Peabody & Stearns and built on this site in 1888.

The Globe National Bank was organized as a state bank in 1824 and became a national bank in 1865. Its nine-story building was built in 1895 at 92 State Street. On the right is the Richards Building, the earliest surviving cast-iron building in the city. Manufactured in Italy, it was erected in 1867 and was named for liquor merchant Calvin A. Richards. The building was remodeled in the 1880s with the addition of two stories that had fanciful pyramidal roofed oriels. The Globe National Bank failed in 1899.

The Tremont National Bank was incorporated in 1814 and became a national bank in 1865. Its headquarters in 1895 were at the corner of Congress and State Streets in a narrow five-story granite building adjacent to the Merchants Exchange at 53 State Street. The bank was absorbed by the Eliot National Bank in 1898. The building was later demolished and replaced by the State Street Trust Company Building, which was designed by Parker, Thomas & Rice and built in 1928 adjacent to the Boston Stock Exchange at 30 Congress Street. The Boston Stock Exchange building was designed by Peabody & Stearns and built in 1908.

The Merchants National Bank was organized in 1831 and became a national bank in 1864. This impressive building with Ionic pilasters supporting a cornice and a modified mansard roof was located at 28 State Street. The bank, which subsequently became the New England Merchants Bank and later the Bank of New England, is today Fleet Bank. Over the last century, it has absorbed the State National Bank in 1912, the National Bank of Commerce in 1914, the Winthrop National Bank in 1915, and the Old Boston National Bank in 1916.

The interior of the Merchants National Bank had wood-paneled and glass teller's windows on the left, with an impressive bracketed cornice supporting a second-floor balcony.

The National Bank of the Republic was organized in 1860 and located at 95 Milk Street. Here, looking from an office with a paper-filled desk, the three men facing the camera are, from left to right, Charles A. Vialle, president; Albert Stone, vice president; and Henry D. Forbes, cashier. The National Bank of the Republic absorbed the National Shawmut Bank in 1908.

The offices of Blodget, Merritt & Company were located at 16 Congress Street. Tellers are at work behind a bronze teller's screen on the left. Glass-domed private wires can be seen on the right.

The International Trust Company was incorporated in 1879. Its headquarters were designed by William Gibbons Preston and built in 1893 at 45 Milk Street at the corner of Devonshire Street. The impressive building was designed with symbolical statuary on its facades by Max Bachman. Safe-deposit vaults were built in the basement under the direct supervision of the New York expert, Mossman.

The lobby to the safe-deposit vaults in the International Trust Company was elaborately decorated with a Venetian mosaic panel with classical figures flanking a cartouche that simply stated, "Fidelity, Security, Trust." The half archway leads to the vaults, which were in the basement of the building.

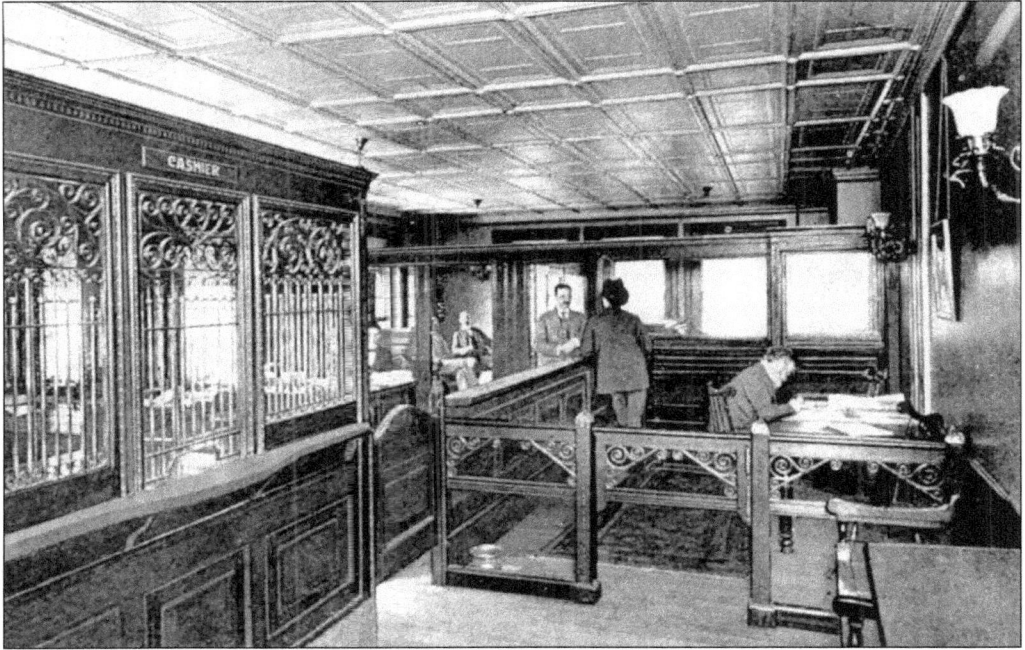

The offices of Mills & Blanchard were located in the Devonshire Building (16 State Street), where they were a banking concern that specialized in municipal bonds. Here, a clerk converses with a client in the office, which has an oriental carpet and the ever present brass spittoon in the center, where it proved most convenient.

The Eastern Banking Company offices were located at 43 Milk Street. The president of the bank, Francis A. Osborn, can be seen in the foreground, seated at his oak roll-top desk. The leather-topped board table can also be seen in the foreground.

The Mount Vernon National Bank was incorporated in 1860 and became a national bank in 1865. It was located at 43 Chauncey Street, just west of Summer Street. Here, an elegant horse-drawn carriage with a top-hatted coachman pulls up in front of the bank in 1895. At that time, the president of the bank was Thomas Nast Hart, a former mayor of Boston. The Mount Vernon National Bank was absorbed by the Boylston National Bank in 1905.

The Shoe and Leather National Bank was incorporated in 1836 and became a national bank in 1865. As its name suggests, it specialized in the banking and finance of the leather industry. The Shoe and Leather National Bank was absorbed by the National Bank of Redemption in 1901.

The Worthington Building was designed by Carl Fehmer and built in 1894 as a 10-story office building at the corner of State and Congress Streets. It stood opposite the Old State House and the site of the Boston Massacre of 1770. A foursquare and solid building, its height and narrowness uses the space well. On the right can be seen Brazers Block, a three-story Greek Revival building with a granite facade that curved toward Devonshire Street on the right; it would eventually be replaced by the Brazer Building, designed by Cass Gilbert and built in 1896.

The offices of Leland, Towle & Company were located in the Worthington Building. The company provided banking and brokerage service to clients. The gallery offices that had velvet portieres that could be pulled closed for privacy—the precursor to office doors.

The Hornblower & Weeks Building was designed by the noted architectural firm of Andrews, Jacques & Rantoul and built in 1908 at the corner of Congress and Water Streets. A six-story stone building of well-proportioned lines and symmetry, it was built with a steel frame and faced with light Bedford limestone with its facade having "been treated with simplicity, the object being to attract attention not by an abundance of decoration, but rather by its absence." Hornblower & Weeks, a partnership of Henry Hornblower and J.W. Weeks, was a leading investment house in the nation with offices not just in Boston, but also in New York and Chicago. The company was a prominent member of both the Boston and New York Stock Exchanges.

The offices of Hornblower & Weeks, seen here at the turn of the century, were equipped with what was then considered modern ledger desks, wood file cabinets, and grills that locked for the protection of the cashiers and safe-deposit vault, the steel door of which is seen on the left. The partners were Mr. Hornblower and John Wingate Weeks (1860–1926).

The offices of Haight & Freese, at 35 State Street, provided comfortable armchairs for those interested in the daily fluctuations of the New York Stock Exchange, which was updated by clerks on the bronze panel seen on the right. Here, the stock, grain, and cotton exchanges and the news tickers are seen in the Boston office in 1895. The news tickers, seen between the windows, had a private wire to the exchanges in Philadelphia, Baltimore, Washington, and Chicago and provided the bankers and commission brokers with up-to-date financial information.

Paine, Webber & Company was founded by William Alfred Paine and Mr. Webber and was located at 52 Devonshire Street. The company was a prominent investment brokerage company that was a member of both the New York and Boston Stock Exchanges.

The office of Cushman, Fisher & Phelps at 50 State Street was comfortably furnished with oak roll top desks, oriental scatter rugs laid over large carpets, and bentwood armchairs, with gasoliers to light the offices. The company specialized in the sale of high-grade bonds.

The offices of E.H. Rollins & Son were located at the State Street Exchange Building at 53 State Street. They were bankers and dealers in municipal bonds, and their office had tellers on the right with a mounted moose head adorning the office wall in the center.

Parkinson & Burr was established in 1866 by partners John Parkinson and I. Tucker Burr. It was a banking and brokerage company located in the State Street Exchange at 53 State Street. The company was a prominent member of both the Boston and New York Stock Exchanges.

The offices of R.L. Day & Company were located at 40 Water Street. A well-known banking and brokerage company, it later merged with Tucker, Anthony & Company.

The International Trust Company, which was founded in 1879, was designed by William Gibbons Preston and built of Indiana limestone in 1892 at the corner of Milk and Devonshire Streets. Preston, a noted architect who had been designing buildings in Boston for well over four decades, designed an impressive eight-story office building with arched windows on the third, seventh, and eighth floors. The other floors were composed of windows set between vertically attenuated engaged columns that intensify the building's height. Preston used Beaux Arts–inspired figures on the face, which represented Commerce, Industry, Security, and Fidelity and were carved by the noted sculptor Max Bachman. On the far left can be seen a corner of the Equitable Life Insurance Building.

The Boston architectural firm of Little & Brown sketched the planned interior remodeling of the International Trust Building that took place in 1905. Little & Brown used high-style Beaux Arts details, such as richly figured marble Doric columns, geometrically inset marble floors, and arches that supported a center glass mullioned dome on pendentive. With richly carved details, cameo profiles, and decorative bronze teller screens, the remodeling proved to be a breathtaking addition to the building, which was also doubled in size. The International Trust Company absorbed the Lincoln Trust in 1914, the Dorchester Trust in 1921, the Old South Trust in 1921, the Hyde Park Trust in 1921, and the Market Trust of Brighton in 1922.

The lobby of the International Trust Company, in a photograph from the *Boston Architectural Club Yearbook* for 1906, shows the marble banking tables on the left with the richly carved and figured Beaux Arts details. Notice the clock flanked by carved fruit cornucopias set in the arch above the teller's cage. In 1923, the International Trust Company was absorbed by the First National Bank of Boston.

The Merchants National Bank was incorporated as a national bank in 1864, and this building was built at 28 State Street, across from the Old State House. On the left is Washington Street, a portion from State to Brattle Street that was discontinued in the mid-1960s, when the area was redeveloped for Boston City Hall Plaza. On the far left can be seen a corner of the Ames Building, which was a Romanesque Revival building designed by Shepley, Rutan & Coolidge.

The State Street Bank and Trust Company was located at 33 State Street in the Worthington Building, an improbably tall building designed by Carl Fehmer and set on a very small lot at the corner of State and Congress Streets. Today, the Bank of Greece is located on the first floor of this elegant but narrow office building.

The Boston Safe Deposit and Trust Company was founded in 1867 and was originally located after 1875 in the basement of the New England Mutual Life Insurance Company in Post Office Square. The present building was designed by Shepley, Rutan & Coolidge and built in 1908–1911 on Franklin Street between Arch and Devonshire Streets. The facade had large arched windows on the street level with a gently curving facade. There are fantastic Conquistador black figured lighting fixtures projecting from the facade that hold lamps that lighted the sidewalk. Today, this is the headquarters of the Boston Stock Exchange.

The New England Trust Company was founded in 1871 and was in a beautiful structure of white Indiana limestone at the corner of Milk and Devonshire Streets. Said to have been "one of the solid, financial institutions of Boston," it was also the oldest trust company in the Commonwealth of Massachusetts and a well-known concern throughout New England.

The Federal Reserve Bank of Boston was designed by R. Clipston Sturgis (1860–1951) and built in 1922 at the corner of Pearl and Franklin Streets. It was organized in 1914 and still serves most of New England. An act of Congress in 1927 deemed that the bank was to have a succession until dissolved by an act of Congress or until forfeiture of its franchise for violation of the law. Sturgis designed the bank in granite and limestone as a rusticated Renaissance Revival building modeled after the Palazzo della Cancellaria in Rome. A flagpole on the cantilevered side of the building was surmounted by a bronze American eagle as a finial. The building of a new Federal Reserve Bank in Dewey Square in 1977 made this building superfluous, and it was subsequently renovated with a new glass mansard roof by Jung, Brannan Associates in 1981. It is now Le Meridien, an elegant hotel.

The banking room of the Federal Reserve Bank of Boston was designed by R. Clipston Sturgis with bold and impressive details. With limestone walls, the interior was as dramatic as it was impressive with massive Corinthian pilasters set on plinth bases with coved arches pointing toward a ceiling skylight. The lobby and lounge of the hotel has N.C. Wyeth murals, marble door frames and mantles, and a gilded, coffered ceiling. Today, through the renovations by Jung, Brannan Associates, the banking room survives as Julien's, the elegantly sumptuous dining room of Le Meridien Hotel. It was named for Julien's Restorator, a restaurant opened by Monsieur Julien, an exile from the French Revolution.

The Provident Institution for Savings was located in a former rowhouse at 36 Temple Place, between Tremont and Washington Streets. The house was purchased by the bank in 1854 from Samuel Cabot, Thomas Cary, William H. Gardiner, and William F. Cary, who were trustees of the estate of the great "merchant prince" Thomas Handasyd Perkins (1764–1854). The house, remodeled by Nathaniel J. Bradlee and built of red brick and granite, was typical of the residences built in this area in the early decades of the 19th century. It remains today as a survivor of a now lost architectural style in the downtown area. In 1933, the bank was renovated by James A. Purdon.

The Old Colony Trust Company was, at the time of the 1920s, "one of the largest, best-known banking institutions in New England." Located at 17 Court Street, its headquarters were composed of deep-set windows punctuating a limestone facade. The bronze-and-glass awning over the front entrance relieved the severely plain facade, as did the bronze tracery separating the first- and second-floor window grills on either side.

The Suffolk Savings Bank for Seamen and Others—or the Boston Five Cents Savings Bank, as it became known in the 20th century—was built in 1926 as a modern building at the corner of School and Province Streets. Designed by the noted Boston architectural firm of Parker Thomas & Rice, the first two floors had engaged Ionic columns supporting a broad cornice that was engraved with the bank's name. The upper floor was composed of paired windows with a dentiled roof cornice. The potted standard shrubs in the foreground decorated the forecourt of Boston's city hall on School Street. Today, the former bank is used as Border's Books and Music, and the modern facade facing Washington Street was added by Kallman & McKinnell in 1972.

The interior of the main office of the Suffolk Savings Bank had a curved marble counter with limestone interior walls and square pilasters. Although the bank had an addition built on the Washington Street facade in 1972, which was designed by Kallman & McKinnell, the interior retains many of the classical details, although it has been remodeled for a major bookstore.

The State Street Bank and Trust Company was founded in 1891, and its headquarters were designed by Parker, Thomas & Rice and built at the corner of Congress and State Streets. A five-story building, it had a heavily rusticated base with a classical Georgian Revival facade that was only two bays wide. The building was flanked the Merchants Exchange at 53 State Street and the Boston Stock Exchange at 30 Congress Street.

The banking floor of the State Street Bank and Trust Company was designed by the architectural firm of Richardson, Barott & Richardson. The bank, headed by Allan Forbes, used reproductions of Colonial furniture and decorative arts for bank patrons to use while transacting business. The walls were adorned with ship-modeled half-hulls and the fabled print collection of the bank. The architects used classical details for the interior reeded columns with a wood-paneled ceiling and summer and cross beams, all of which added to the distinct charm of the interior.

103

The Suffolk National Savings Bank was founded in 1818 and became a national bank in 1865; it was located at the corner of Tremont Street and Pemberton Square. An impressive bank built of granite, the four bold recessed Doric columns created an impressive facade. On the far left can be seen a corner of the Hemenway Building, designed by Nathaniel J. Bradlee and built at the corner of Tremont and Court Streets. Today, the site of the Suffolk Savings Bank is Center Plaza, which was designed by Welton Beckett and Associates and built in 1965.

The Second Federal Savings Bank was formerly the Second National (Granite) Bank. It was founded in 1833 and became a national bank in 1864. The Colonial Revival building was designed by the Boston architectural firm of Holmes & Edwards and built at 19 School Street. The modified Palladian window on the second floor, symmetry of the facade, inset carved panels, and heavily bracketed cornice and balustrade all make for an impressive pre–World War II facade.

Six

Lunch-Hour Shopping

The numerous department stores of Boston's financial district have offered quality goods and merchandise in palace-sized stores, which had clerks who offered service at a moment's notice.

In the 19th century, Boston had numerous shops and small stores that offered both domestic and imported merchandise for the shoppers who thronged the stores six days a week. However, by the late 19th century, Boston began to see what were to become institutions opened that would, in some cases, serve generations of Bostonians. Among the early stores were C.F. Hovey & Company, which was on Summer Street opposite Hawley Street, Jordan Marsh & Company at the corner of Washington and Summer Streets, Gilchrist's at the corner of Washington and Winter Streets, and William Filene & Son at the corner of Summer and Washington Streets. These four department stores, all within a short distance of one another, represented the core of what is today referred to as Downtown Crossing. However, there were other stores that also offered quality merchandise.

Raymond's, Houghton & Dutton, Leopold Morse & Company, Shuman & Company, Conrad & Chandler's, Coleman's, and other well-patronized stores were all located in Boston's financial district. Although open throughout the day and on certain evenings, they were thronged with lunch-hour shoppers from the hundreds of businesses in the area. Lunch-hour shopping became the time for a quick errand, an advertised bargain, or even an impromptu visit to Filene's Basement for a quick look at its sale extravaganzas.

Jordan Marsh & Company was established in 1841 by Eben Dyer Jordan and Benjamin L. Marsh at the corner of Washington and Summer Streets. The department store was the largest of its kind in New England and had 66 departments, 3,500 employees, and 15 acres of floor space in a massive building that was designed by the noted Boston architectural firm of Winslow & Wetherall, successors to Nathaniel J. Bradlee. In 1949, an addition designed by the noted architectural firm of Perry, Shaw & Hepburn was built on Summer Street on the site of the C.F. Hovey & Company. Today, the store is known as Macy's, a branch of the New York store that was established by Rowland Hussey Macy, a Nantucket native who moved to Manhattan to pursue a business career.

Eben Dyer Jordan and Benjamin L. Marsh were pioneers in modern methods of merchandising and were considered to be among the greatest merchants in the United States, as well as benevolent employers and supporters of numerous charitable endeavors and worthy causes.

Filene's was established in 1852 by William Filene. His son was Edward Albert Filene (1860–1937), who moved the store from Salem to the city in 1881. He eventually commissioned Chicago architect Daniel Burnham (1846–1912) to build his department store at the corner of Washington and Summer Streets in 1911. Filene's business policy was to include his employees in a progressive, employee-owned corporation that instituted paid vacations, an employee credit union, and profit sharing, which would hopefully propel employees to excel in annual sales. The massive classically interpreted store had a rooftop recreation field, an employee hospital, a library, and a meeting hall, in addition to a fine dining room for shoppers.

A view looking up Summer Street toward Washington Street from Miner, Beal & Company, at the corner of Chauncey Street, shows Filene's with its gently curving facade in the center of the photograph. Gilchrist's, designed by Bigelow & Wadsworth and built in 1912, is to its left at the corner of Washington and Winter Streets, and Kennedy's is on its right. Filene was an innovator who invented the automatic markdown system that made Filene's Basement, a Boston institution that was advertised as being "better known and far more often visited than Fanueil Hall or the Old State House."

The R.H. White Department Store was designed by Peabody and Stearns and built in 1877 at 518–538 Washington Street in the theater district. Noted for its fine household goods, it was one of numerous department stores like Conrad & Chandler and Coleman's Fashion Shop that are today still fondly remembered by many Bostonians.

The ladies' parlor in the R.H. White Department Store was designed by Peabody and Stearns with a massive working fireplace, which was recessed into a broad Romanesque arch that was faced in marble with glazed tiles and carved stone. Notice the clock set in the arch above the fireplace and the fantastic wrought andirons, all of which made this parlor an elegant and relaxing place for ladies to gather themselves after an afternoon of shopping.

The R.H. Stearns Department Store was designed by the Boston architectural firm of Parker, Thomas & Rice and built in 1912 at the corner of Tremont Street and Temple Place on the site of the old Masonic Temple. Today, the building has stores on the street floor and senior apartments above. On the left can be seen the Ionic-columned temple facade of St. Paul's Church, which has remained unchanged for almost two centuries and is a stabilizing factor of the Tremont Street streetscape.

The Houghton & Dutton Department Store was located in the Albion Building, which was at the corner of Tremont and Beacon Streets. The Albion Building was designed by Cummings and Sears and built in 1888 opposite the King's Chapel and its burying ground. An impressive multistoried building, it was adjacent to the Suffolk County Court House on Pemberton Square and attracted numerous loyal patrons. Today, the site of the Albion Building is 1 Beacon Place, a high-rise office building designed by Skidmore, Owings & Merrill and built in 1972.

This four-story building at the corner of Washington and Winter Streets was Filene's Baby and Miss Annex, where in 1890 William and Edward A. Filene had relocated and set up shop before building in 1912 the landmark department store diagonally across the street. On the left is the Ditson Building, which was built in 1900 for the Oliver Ditson Music Publishing Company. These facades survive today and are important examples of the low-rise buildings of Downtown Crossing.

The Walker-Stetson-Sawyer Company was located in a six-story building at 69 Bedford Street, where it offered hosiery, underwear, laces, kid gloves, knit goods, ladies' wrappers, art embroidery goods, and gentlemen's furnishings. It offered a "three-horse hitch," which was to be translated as "style, quality, and price," all of which worked in unison to pull its "commercial barouche to success."

Leopold Morse & Company was established in 1852 by Jacob Morse, Ferdinand Strauss, and Louis Strauss and was located in a five-story building at the corner of Washington and Brattle Streets in Adams Square, now a part of City Hall Plaza. Morse & Company, once the oldest retail clothing house in Boston, offered wholesale and retail clothing for men and boys. The side oriel had a three-sided clock that was a landmark in this area for almost a century. In the foreground is the bronze statue of Samuel Adams (1722–1803), patriot, governor of the Commonwealth of Massachusetts, and beer brewer. The statue was sculpted by Anne Whitney and is today in front of Fanueil Hall, facing the former Dock Square.

Leopold Morse (1831–1892) was the son of one of the founders of the Leopold Morse Company and "raised his enterprise into one of the largest and most important of its line in the city." Morse was not just owner of this large department store, but he served as a member of the House of Representatives for a decade. He was a benefactor of the Morse Home for Aged and Infirm Hebrews and Orphanage, which was opened in 1889 in the former Cornell-Austin mansion on Mattapan Street (now Blue Hills Parkway) in Milton and remained until 1914, when it was moved to Dorchester.

C.F. Hovey & Company, which had been founded in 1842, was an old-line department store at Summer and Chauncey Streets. Hovey & Company were importers, jobbers, and retailers of dry goods and offered dress goods, silks, shawls, and a full line of ladies and children's garments. Hovey's was "one of the acknowledged leading wholesale and retail dry goods houses in New England and one of the largest in the United States."

Raymond's Department Store was located on Washington Street between Franklin and Summer Streets. One of many department stores, Raymond's adopted Uncle Eph and Aunt Abby as its trademark, and its "Yankee common sense" translated into reasonable prices. Raymond's, however, moved farther up Washington Street near Milk and then eventually down Washington Street opposite West Street before it closed in the 1960s.

Seven

BETWEEN THE WARS

With the erection in 1915 of the Boston Custom House tower on top of the original Greek Revival building that had been completed in 1849, Boston's financial district had its first true skyscraper. The tower, designed by the noted architectural firm of Peabody & Stearns, was a steel-frame structure sheathed in granite. It was completed just as the war began in Europe, which would eventually induce America to enter World War I. Between World War I and World War II, there was a dramatic decrease in building in the city compared to the 50 years previous to 1915.

In the period between 1872 (when the financial district was destroyed by fire) and World War I, the area of Boston's financial district was rebuilt with hundreds of new buildings in a business-zoned area. However by the 1920s, the area was largely built up and there was relatively little new building. The most notable buildings in this period were the United Shoe Machinery Company and the Batterymarch Building, both of which took into account the new Boston zoning law, which had been enacted by the Boston City Planning Board. The waterfront, which in the 19th century had been infilled from the area of Dock Square east to provide new streets and buildable land, had become less active. The Commonwealth Pier (now the World Trade Center), where large ocean liners docked after 1913, had been moved due to the depth of the harbor. The numerous fishing concerns and fish boats that once docked along the waterfront began to relocate, or go out of business completely, and this occurrence changed the once thriving and vibrant waterfront into a stagnant and oddly changed area. The Great Depression was to severely affect not just the economy of the country, but also to begin the decline in the waterfront and the building boom of the recent past. With the relocation of the produce market from Quincy Market to Everett and Chelsea and the meat market to the area of South Bay in Roxbury, great changes took place in the usage of a once busy marketplace. The building of the Southeast Expressway through the area in the 1950s further impacted the density of land usage and effectively cut off the North End and the waterfront from the financial district.

The erection of a tower above the Greek Revival custom house in 1914–1915 was a major undertaking in the city and one that created the first "skyscraper" in Boston. The custom house was designed by Ammi Burnham Young, assisted by J.H. Hammatt Billings, and built of Quincy granite between 1837 and 1849. The building, with its monolithic granite columns, originally stood on the edge of Boston Harbor, but through infilling in the 19th century, this area was developed for new streets and building lots. When the tower was being constructed, the interior rotunda was removed. The 12 marble Corinthian columns were removed, and 8 were used to create a monumental gateway to the entrance of Franklin Park in Dorchester. Here, the steel framework for the tower is being laid with a derrick on the platform bringing up steel beams.

Seen from the Boston Fish Pier, the Boston Custom House tower has neared its completion in 1915 with half of the shaft already sheathed in granite and the iron framework being completed above. Peabody & Stearns had not only built the first skyscraper in the city, but they used granite that harmonized with the original Greek Revival building and enormous winged eagles on the four corners flanking the four-sided clock.

114

This study of a high-rise office building was done by Kilham, Hopkins & Greeley in 1928 as an example of the new Boston zoning law, which had been enacted by the Boston City Planning Board. The planning board prepared a study of the future growth of the city and the development of plans for improvements to meet the growing needs of traffic, housing, public building sites, and park and playground facilities. In 1928, the board allowed an alternate method of height limits in the 155-foot height district by allowing heights exceeding 155 feet to have setbacks "so that all portions of the building shall be within planes sloping in from all lot and party lines one foot for each two and a half feet in height."

The United Shoe Machinery Company, at 140 Federal Street, was designed by Parker, Thomas & Rice, associated with Henry Bailey Alden, and built in 1928–1930. This trapezoidal Art Deco building took into effect the Boston zoning law, with a greater flexibility in design that was permitted to the architects and a substantial increase in maximum height being permitted on large lots without restricting the light and air of surrounding properties. This was the first Art Deco skyscraper to be built in Boston, and with its base of limestone and dark-black granite, it rose as a tower of brick, stone, and metal in vertical steps to the top, which had a little roof of tiles. The United Shoe Machinery Building has been listed on the National Resister of Historic Places in recognition of its importance in Boston's financial district.

The headquarters of the *Boston Herald Traveler* was remodeled by the Boston architectural firm of Holmes & Edwards. An Art Deco–inspired office building with a modified Gothic-inspired crenellation, it created an interesting three-dimensional quality to the streetscape. The *Boston Herald Traveler*, now known as the *Boston Herald*, was a competitor to other newspapers printed during the 20th century but today is only one of two to survive, its competitor being the *Boston Globe*. The *Boston Globe* moved its operation from Washington Street's Cornhill area, near Milk Street, to Dorchester's Morrissey Boulevard in 1957.

The Public Service Building, or the Batterymarch Building, was designed by Harold Field Kellogg and was built in 1927 at the corner of Batterymarch and Franklin Streets. This Art Deco office building has dark-brown stone-glazed brick piers that lighten in color to buff-colored brick as they rise up the facade and taper toward the top in steps. Insets like Gothic crenellation connect the piers. With shops on the street level of the building, the building is both innovative as well as intriguing in its design. Unfortunately, the Batterymarch Building cannot really be viewed properly due to the narrowness of the street and the density of surrounding buildings; much of its design is unviewable except at an angle.

116

The Eastern Packet Pier is pictured c. 1950 with numerous fishing boats docked at the pier. These boats, among them *Annie & Josie*, *Ethel*, *Acme* and *Saint Anna*, were remnants of the one-time massive fishing fleet that operated out of the Port of Boston. By the time of the Great Depression, most of the small fishing concerns had relocated or closed, and the waterfront began a slow decline. Here, the Boston Custom House tower dominates the waterfront with few buildings challenging its supremacy of height.

Fort Point Channel has a ship passing through the channel as traffic is halted on both sides of the traffic barriers. Named for the inner channel of water that passed Fort Hill, the area was almost completely surrounded through infilling in the late 19th century with this narrow channel surviving for delivery of goods by boat and barge. On the upper left is the United Shoe Machinery Building (at 140 Federal Street), designed by Parker, Thomas & Rice, associated with Henry Bailey Alden in 1928–1930.

117

Downtown Boston had the Boston Custom House tower as its only skyscraper in the mid-20th century. Designed by Peabody & Stearns, the tower surmounted the Greek Revival custom house and created a granite beacon that was recognizable as one approached the city in any direction. In the foreground is the Northern Avenue Bridge, designed by engineer William Jackson and built in 1910. The bridge crosses the Fort Point Channel and connects the city proper and South Boston in an area known as Fort Point. Today, the Southeast Expressway, which cut a wide swath through this area in the 1950s, is being dismantled, and a greenstrip will eventually replace the green metal monster. The former custom house has been converted to an elegant timeshare of Marriott Corporation known as Marriott's Custom House.

The financial district, seen in the post–World War II years, was dominated by the Peabody & Stearns–designed Boston Custom House tower, which was a beacon along the waterfront and the city's only true skyscraper until the old John Hancock Building was built in the Back Bay. In the center can be seen the dome and pavilions of Quincy Market with Fanueil Hall in the foreground. The lower part of the photograph shows the tremendous amount of building that took place in the 1890–1950 period, which stagnated in the post–World War II years.

Eight

TOWARD A
NEW URBANISM

In the last two decades, architecture in Boston has become increasingly more sleek and dense, with taller office buildings being built on smaller lots of land. This chapter tries to identify those buildings that point toward a new urbanism, which is said to "believe that dwellings and other functions should be clustered close together so people can get around by walking instead of driving." The principles pertain to housing, workplaces, stores, entertainment centers, schools, parks, and civic facilities essential to the daily lives of the residents. The car culture of the nation took hold after World War II. In many instances, people living in suburbia cannot get from one point to another without the use of an automobile, let alone to the train and commuter rail, and therefore have maintained suburban sprawl. New urbanism brings together principles required to create mixed-use walkable and diverse neighborhoods that strive to create better and more liveable communities.

However, new urbanism is considered by many to be the most important planning movement of the last few decades. International adherents have conceived of it as a truly 19th-century retrospective, in that everything one might need, or want to do, is (or at least should be) within walking distance of one's home. The principles of new urbanism include walkability, connectivity, mixed usage and diversity, mixed housing, increased density, and most importantly, the sustainability of the quality of life .Of course, the aspect of new neighborhoods that adhere to the new urbanist "ism" ideas does not always echo back to the 19th century. New buildings are often luxury high-rise buildings set in urban sectors that appeal to wealthier residents and empty nesters who flock to the city in their postsuburban lives. New urbanism does strive to revive the lost art of place making and a reevaluation of the built environment. With the decreasing need for an automobile in the city (although most residents of these luxury condominiums keep one), the ideology of high-density developments takes on new meaning. Residents live high above the daily street life and only participate when off to the theater, ballet, or other entertainment, but the benefits to residents, businesses, developers, and the city are immeasurable if zoning is addressed.

The Old State House seems dwarfed by the high-rise office buildings surrounding it. On the left is 15 State Street, the Easton Building, which was built by the Ames Estate, who also built the Ames Building at Court and Washington Streets. One Boston Place, designed by Pietro Belluschi and built in 1970, looms high above the other buildings in this area of the city, creating a density of usage on a small lot of land. (Photograph by James Z. Kyprianos.)

In a view looking west on State Street, the dominant feature of the streetscape is not the Old State House, but 1 Boston Place, at the corner of Washington and Court Streets. Designed by Pietro Belluschi, the high-rise office tower was built with walls of bronze tinted glass and aluminum on the site of the Old Brick Meeting House. The late-19th-century scale of State Street is somewhat maintained by the buildings in the foreground, but by the 1890s, the building of the Fiske Building and the State Street Exchange created a high-rise aspect that has been dwarfed a century later. On the right is the India Building, designed by Peabody & Stearns and built in 1904 at 84 State Street. Also on the right are the oriels of the Richards Building, built in 1867 of cast iron manufactured in Italy and erected at 112 State Street for Calvin A. Richards, a wholesale liquor dealer. (Photograph by James Z. Kyprianos.)

The State Street Exchange, in the center, is flanked by a part of 75 State Street on the left and the looming tower of 1 Beacon Street on the right. Built of rough-hewn granite, the State Street Exchange was designed by Peabody & Stearns to gently curve from Kilby Street onto State Street. Their use of arched windows seems to create a cap to the multistoried office building with regulated windows. The comparison between 75 State Street by Graham Gund Associates, the Peabody & Stearns State Street Exchange, and Pietro Belluschi's 1 Boston Place is interesting, with all built within a century and each representing a unique interpretation of its architect and a diverse architectural style in one area. (Photograph by James Z. Kyprianos.)

The building at 75 State Street was designed by Graham Gund Associates and Skidmore, Owings & Merrill and built in 1988 on the site of the Fiske Building. This office tower, seen from Merchants Row, is a profusely decorated high rise built of granite with gold leaf decoration. With its numerous setbacks as it rises to the top, its bays, and alternating color, it creates a vivid impression on the somewhat staid and somber State Street streetscape. (Photograph by James Z. Kyprianos.)

The Old South Church is dwarfed by the Devonshire on the left, designed by Steffian Bradley Associates and built in 1982, and 60 State Street on the right of its Colonial spire, designed by Skidmore, Owings & Merrill and built in 1977. Built in 1729, the Old South Church survives on Washington Street in Boston's financial district as a poignant reminder of the city's rich Colonial past, but with an eye to the future. On the far right can be seen a corner of the Transcript Building, which was designed by Gridley J. Fox Bryant and built in 1873 for the *Boston Transcript*, a leading newspaper of the 19th century and where the largest daily in New England was published, in quarto form, in the late 19th century. (Photograph by James Z. Kyprianos.)

In a view looking west on Summer Street, the Church Green Building acts as a skirt to the tower of 99 Summer Street, which was designed by Goody, Clancy & Associates and built in 1986. Built of grey granite, its facade imitates the earlier 1873 building designed by Jonathan Preston and built after the Great Boston Fire of 1872. The stepped roofline of the tower echoes, in some ways, the mansard-roofed earlier building with its projecting dormers and regimented window placement, all of which create an interesting three-dimensional quality to the ensemble. (Photograph by James Z. Kyprianos.)

The Telephone Building dominates the south side of Post Office Square, fronting on Franklin Street and flanked by Pearl and Congress Streets. A stepped Art Deco building, it was designed by Cram & Ferguson and built in 1947–1952. It has a granite facade with paired windows set between ribbons of stone that accentuate its verticality. (Photograph by James Z. Kyprianos.)

A view looking south at Post Office Square shows the Telephone Building (right), which was designed by Cram & Ferguson and built in 1947–1952 on the site of the Mutual Life Insurance Company of New York and the New England Mutual Life Insurance Company, which were designed by Peabody & Stearns and Nathaniel J. Bradlee, respectively. On the far left is the State Street Bank, a high-relief precast concrete high rise designed by the Pearl Street Associates and built in 1966. In the center is 125 High Street, designed by Jung, Brannan and built in 1991. It is an interesting development that incorporates 19th-century buildings on Oliver and Purchase Streets as a skirt with a station of the Boston Fire Department as well. In the foreground is a lush and inviting garden that was designed by the Halverson Company, a landscape architectural firm, and Ellenzeig Associates, architects, who have joined efforts to create an oasis in the center of Post Office Square with the ever useful and highly used multilevel parking garage located underground.

On the north side of Post Office Square, the John McCormack Post Office can be seen on the left. Designed by Cram & Ferguson with James A. Wetmore and built in 1931, this granite Art Deco building has a streamline look with Gothic overtones. Exchange Place and 60 State Street can be seen in the center with the dual bay 125 High Street building and 1 Post Office Square on the right.

Post Office Square is dominated by the Telephone Building on the left, but the Keystone Building and the Fleet Bank Building can be seen on the right. The Keystone Building was designed by Pietro Belluschi and built in 1970 for the Keystone Custodian Funds. It is a tower of white marble and identical rows of windows that flare out from each individual bay. The Fleet Bank Building is an odd-shaped building, often referred to as the "pregnant building." Designed by Campbell, Aldrich & Nulty with Carl A. Morse Inc. as consultant and built in 1971, the exterior surface is of dark granite, which is quite a color juxtaposition with the lightness of the Keystone Building.

124

Dewey Square, named for Adm. George Dewey (1837–1917) the "hero of Manila," is the junction of Atlantic Avenue and Summer Street. The classically inspired South Station was designed by Shepley, Rutan & Coolidge and built in 1897–1899. The station, a leading connector for Amtrack, the commuter rail, and the Red Line of the MBTA, was restored by Hugh Stubbins & Associates with the public spaces and offices by Stull and Lee. On the left is the Fiduciary Trust Building, designed by the Architects Collaborative with a corner of the Federal Reserve Bank. On the right is 1 Financial Place, a six-sided 45-foot tower that was designed by Pietro Belluschi and Jung, Brannan Associates and built in 1983. The building has a 90-foot atrium that projects from the tower, which has a granite base and a tower of cast stone and glass.

The Fiduciary Trust Building, on the left, was designed by the Architects Collaborative and built of dark-grey concrete at 175 Federal Street in 1977. To its right in the center of the photograph is the Federal Reserve Bank of Boston, a brushed white anodized aluminum high rise designed by Hugh Stubbins & Associates and built in 1972–1977 at 600 Atlantic Avenue. Both of these buildings are eccentric examples of Modernism in Boston, with little exterior embellishments, pared back details, and little, if any, relation to the surrounding buildings of the previous decades. The Fiduciary Trust Building is an irregular hexagon with its upper stories cantilevered on all sides. The Federal Reserve Bank has unique aluminum spandrels, or eyebrow awnings, that might shade the offices from the sun but also create a three-dimensional aspect to the verticality of the building.

This dramatic photograph from Beech Street shows 1 Lincoln Street, which is currently under construction for the State Street Corporation. On its right is 125 Summer Street, which was designed by Kohn, Pederson, Fox and built in 1990. The Fiduciary Trust Building is in the center, with the State Street Bank and Trust Building rising above it. On the far right is Lincoln Plaza, at the corner of Lincoln and Essex Streets, in what is often referred to as the Leather District.

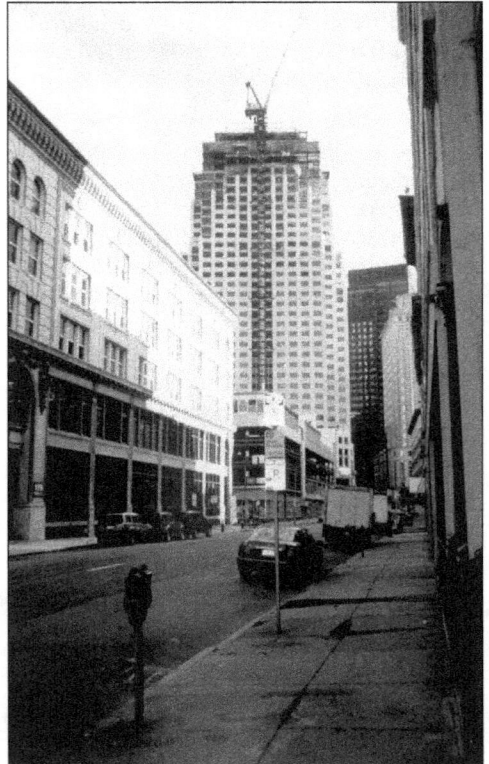

The new building at 1 Lincoln Street rises toward completion. Designed by Jung-Brannan Associates with Tso Associates, it is being built for the State Street Corporation. On the left is the Albany Building at the corner of Kneeland and South Streets, which is now the location for the offices of Teradyne.

The area of Dock Square has seen great changes in the height of new office buildings. Fanueil Hall and Quincy Market seem dwarfed by the new Marketplace Center, a 16-story glass tower designed by WZMH Group and built in 1985 at State and Commercial Streets. Marketplace Center is seen in the center with its pyramidal roof and granite-and-glass facade. One of the Harbor towers rises to the left of the Boston Custom House, seen just above Fanueil Hall. In the foreground, the sloping glass greenhouse roofs are Exotic Flowers, which was designed by Benjamin Thompson Associates and creates an interesting modernistic juxtaposition with the older buildings in the area. (Photograph by James Z. Kyprianos.)

In a view looking east on Boylston Street from Charles Street West, the Residences are the new high rises of the Ritz Carlton Hotel. The hotel can be seen in the distance, rising above the Masonic Temple of the Grand Lodge of Masons, which was designed by Merrill G. Wheelock at the corner of Tremont and Boylston Streets. The Residences, the Ritz Carlton Suites on the right, and the hotel and towers on the left, offer luxury living high above the transformed area between Tremont and Washington Streets, now referred to as the theater district but formerly known as the Combat Zone.

State Street, seen in a view looking west toward the Old State House in 1895, had the remnants of early brick and granite commercial buildings interspersed with newer and taller Victorian commercial blocks that had greatly changed the character, as well as the scale, of the area. In many ways, the Old State House seems dwarfed by these high-rise buildings (only a century after the scene had been painted), and Boston's financial district took on a decidedly banking and insurance connotation that would remain well into the 20th century. Broad Street can be seen on the left with the Foreign Fruit Store doing business in an early-19th-century brick building on the corner. The Fiske Building and the State Street Exchange are farther up State Street. On the right can be seen the facade of the cast-iron Richards Building (with a wall sign for the Commercial Cable Company) with its twin two-story oriels at the top.

For J.B. Price.

ACKNOWLEDGMENTS

Sincere thanks go the following people who contributed in some way, either directly or indirectly, in the research, writing, and editing of this photographic history: Jill Anderson, my ever patient editor; William Belliveau; the Boston Public Library; Frank Cheney; Elise M. Ciregna and Stephen Lo Piccolo; Dexter; Edward W. Gordon; Helen Hannon; Sally Ann Kydd; James Z. Kyprianos; Susan Wood Paine; Rev. Michael J. Parise; William H. Pear; Sally Pierce of the Boston Athenaeum, Print Room; Anthony and Mary Mitchell Sammarco; the Urban College of Boston; and William Varrell. Unless otherwise noted, photographs are from the author's collection.

www.ingramcontent.com/pod-product-compliance
Lightning Source LLC
Chambersburg PA
CBHW050652150426
42813CB00055B/1372